Discounting Teamwork

These days, virtually no one will tell you that teamwork isn't important when it comes to an organization achieving its goals. Even cynics understand that groups of people who are willing to put their individual interests aside for the good of the team will outperform groups of people who do not.

Having said that, there is something that often happens after a team succeeds that suggests many of us might be discounting the real power of teamwork. A great example of this happens in the world of professional sports.

With the football season just behind us, perhaps a hypothetical example from the NFL would be a good case study. Imagine that a team wins the Super Bowl with less talent than many of the teams it defeated along the way. This is not all that uncommon in sports—the San Francisco Giants of this past baseball season and the New England Patriots of recent years come to mind. When this happens, television announcers, journalists, coaches and sports executives often rave about the amazing culture of teamwork that existed, and how it was what allowed the team to over-achieve and beat the odds.

Those people seem sincere when they make that claim, but then something strange happens during the off-season which doesn't really make sense. As soon as the free-agent market opens up and executives try to sign new players or make trades with other organizations, a premium is placed on athletes who played for the championship team. General managers are suddenly willing to bid higher and pay more to pry a linebacker or wide-receiver away from the Super Bowl team, as though they are now more valuable. All too often, those same general managers find themselves disappointed the following season when the new recruit doesn't do for his new team what he apparently did for his old one.

Of course, the explanation for this is obvious: the culture of teamwork that the Super Bowl champ created made its players much more effective than they would have been on other teams. As a result, the collective achievement of the team exceeded what anyone would have been able to predict based on an individual analysis of talent.

Now, if we really believed in the power of that team culture, then we would know that taking someone off that team and putting them in a new organization is going to have a profound impact on their performance. And so the question is, do those executives really believe what they said about teamwork and somehow forget it in their desire to find new players, or do they just give lip-service to teamwork and deep down inside believe it all comes down to talent?

This same phenomenon also happens in business. Companies spend a lot of time and energy trying to acquire talent from successful organizations, believing that by doing so, they'll be able to improve the performance of their own organizations. In most situations, people from great companies aren't easy to lure away from healthy, successful organizations, and so they command higher salaries. Unfortunately, like in the NFL, the return on investment is rarely what the acquiring company was striving for.

What's the practical lesson for companies trying to improve? They should start by spending more of their time and effort creating a culture of teamwork than looking for outside talent, because the rewards for doing so are enormous. For starters, they'll get more from the employees they already have, and even find stars who are already in their midst. Remember, great football teams birth superstars from the ranks of ordinary players who happen to have extraordinary attitudes. Beyond that, companies that create true team environments become places where other team-oriented players want to work. Great football teams attract players who are tired of playing for selfish, dysfunctional teams, and, in many cases, they even play for less money to have that opportunity.

Also by Patrick Lencioni

CONTENTS

A Note from Pat

The book you're holding is a collection of short essays I've written over the years on an array of topics related to organizational life. I hope you enjoy them.

Many of these ideas were originally shared with readers via our Point-of-View program, which is a series of pieces that my company, The Table Group, regularly e-mails to our readers and clients. Several entries were also published in other media outlets. Whatever the case, the essays here go beyond what I've written in my books, covering issues ranging from innovation to virtual teams to something I call adrenaline addiction.

My goal in writing these POVs is always to be practical, interesting and concise, and to provoke readers to think about how they might be able to more positively impact the lives of the people they lead and manage. I hope these ideas resonate with you in some way.

Pat Lencioni

If you're interested in receiving Pat's complimentary POV, please visit www.tablegroup.com to sign up.

Perhaps the first thing that a company needs to do in order to improve is to ask itself if it truly believes that teamwork is a strategic advantage, and that it, more than shear talent, brings about lasting success.

― FEBRUARY 2011

The content from this article was based on Pat's book, *The Five Dysfunctions of a Team*. For more on the book, the model and free tools, please visit www.tablegroup.com.

Stooping to Greatness

Earlier this year I had the opportunity to spend time with the CEO of one of America's most successful companies, a legendary organization known for its employee and customer satisfaction, as well as its financial performance. I attended their company's management conference, listened to various presentations about their culture, and the extraordinary, homey and sometimes slightly wacky practices that distinguish them from their competitors.

Overwhelmed by the organization's simple and powerful behavioral philosophy, I asked the CEO a semi-rhetorical question. "Why in the world don't your competitors do any of this?" The CEO thought about it for a moment and said, "You know, I honestly believe they think it's beneath them."

And right away, I knew he was right.

After all, every one of those competitors, the vast majority of whom are struggling, knows exactly what this company does, how it works, and how much it has driven its financial success. The company's cultural approach has been chronicled in more than a few books. And yet, none of them tries to emulate it. In fact, based on numerous interactions I've had with employees who work for those competitors, I'd have to say that their attitude is often dismissive, even derisive, toward this company and its enthusiastic employees.

And this dynamic exists in other industries, too. A quick-service company I know has remarkable customer loyalty, as well as unbelievable employee satisfaction and retention, especially compared to the majority of their competitors. The leaders and employees of the company attribute most of their success to the behavioral philosophy and attitude that they've cultivated within the organization, and the unconventional yet effective activities that result.

One example of that philosophy is the action of the CEO, who shows up at grand openings of new franchises where he stays up all night with employees, playing instruments and handing out food to excited customers. Few CEOs would be happy, or even willing, to do things like this, but this executive relishes the opportunity. These, and other activities that most MBAs would call corny, are precisely what makes that company unique.

This happens in the world of sports, as well. There is a well-known high school football team where I live that is ranked near the top of national polls every year. They play the best teams in the country, teams with bigger and more highly touted players, and beat them regularly. The secret to their success, more than any game strategy or weight-lifting regimen, comes down to the coach's philosophy about commitment and teamwork and the buy-in he gets from his players. That philosophy manifests itself in a variety of simple actions which speak to how the players treat one another on and off the field. For example, players pair up every week and exchange 3x5 cards with hand-written commitments around training and personal improvement, and then take responsibility for disciplining one another when those commitments aren't met.

And yet, whenever I explain this and similar practices of the team to other coaches who are curious about their success, I encounter that same sense of dismissiveness. They get a look on their face that seems to say, "listen, I'm not going to do that. It's silly. Just tell me something technical that I can use." As a result, few teams actually try to copy them. Some skeptics might say, "come on, those companies/teams are successful because they're good at what they do." And they'd be right. Those organizations are undoubtedly and extremely competent in their given fields, and they have to be in order to succeed. But plenty of other organizations are just as competent and don't achieve great levels of success, and I honestly believe it's because they're unwilling to stoop down and do the simple, emotional, home-spun things that all human beings—employees, customers, players—really crave.

What's at the heart of this unwillingness? I think it's pride. Though plenty of people in the world say they want to be successful, not that many are willing to humble themselves and do the simple things that might seem unsophisticated. Essentially, they come to define success by what people think of them, rather than by what they accomplish, which is ironic because they often end up losing the admiration of their employees and customers/fans.

The good news in all of this is that for those organizations that want to succeed more than they want to maintain some artificial sense of professionalism (whatever that means), there is great opportunity for competitive advantage and success. They can create a culture of performance and service and employee engagement, the kind that ensures long term success like no strategy ever could. But only if they're willing to stoop down and be human, to treat their customers and one another in ways that others might find corny.

— DECEMBER 2010

The Dilemma of the Difficult Employee

It's a simple but painful problem that has plagued business people since the beginning of time, I'm sure. From shopkeepers in ancient Rome to English factory supervisors during the Industrial Revolution to software engineering managers in modern Silicon Valley, leaders have always struggled with the question of what to do about a difficult employee. And the dilemma is almost always seen the same way: should I continue to tolerate this person or let them go?

The first step toward solving this simple and painful problem is coming to the realization that it is a false dilemma. The decision should not boil down to keeping or firing a difficult employee. In fact, the manager should avoid engaging in this line of thinking in the first place. The real question a manager needs to ask is "have I done everything I can to help the difficult employee?" Based on my work with leaders in all types of organizations and at all levels, the answer to that question is usually a resounding 'no.' Here's what I mean.

Most managers—including me during much of my career—react the same way when they come to the realization that one of their people is a problem. First, they find someone to vent to about it. Usually to a colleague, sometimes to a subordinate, and almost always their spouse. On a courageous day, they might make a subtle comment to the difficult employee, or if they're timing is lucky, be able to include something in an upcoming employee review. What they rarely do is sit down with that employee and tell them, in no uncertain terms, that their attitude needs to change.

As ridiculously obvious as that sounds, and as much sense as it makes to anyone who has ever coached little league or parented a child, it rarely happens. Whether it is a CEO dealing with an arrogant or condescending VP of sales, a pastor managing a rude church receptionist, or a school principal hearing complaints about a caustic teacher, very few leaders have the guts to directly and unequivocally let a difficult employee know that their behavior is patently unacceptable.

This is understandable given that in many of these situations the employee in question is somewhat of a peer to the leader. No one relishes the idea of having to give a colleague bad news, especially when that news has to do with their personality or behavior. And so it is not surprising that leaders often hesitate, procrastinate, even abdicate their responsibilities, hoping that the situation will somehow change on its own.

But it rarely does, and the complaints continue, and that's when the false dilemma starts to emerge and leaders feel like they have to make a "buy or sell" decision. If they fire the employee, the consequences aren't pretty—there is the potential for a lawsuit or expensive severance, not to mention the possibility of a morale problem among the people who liked the employee or never saw the problematic behavior. And then there is the loss of that person's production and the need to hire a replacement. On the other hand, if the leader decides to keep the difficult employee, there is the inevitable morale problem among the people who experience the poor behavior, and the loss of credibility that the leader will experience for not having the courage to make a hard decision.

And so the manager engages in a stressful and fruitless calculus exercise, constantly trying to estimate and mitigate the damage that either decision will create, all the while watching the stakes grow and grow with every passing day. What that manager needs to do is as fool proof as it is difficult: inform the difficult employee that he is being, well, difficult, and continue to remind him again and again and again until one of three good things happens.

In the best possible scenario, the employee gets so tired of the manager reminding him how difficult he is that he changes his behavior. This is certainly what any manager would prefer, but it cannot happen without honest and incessant communication. In the next best scenario, the employee gets so tired of the manager reminding him how difficult he is that he decides to leave the organization. This allows him to take action on his own terms, and it avoids the stress of lawsuits and the cost of severance.

Even the third and worst case scenario is preferable to the false dilemma that managers put themselves in. If the difficult employee decides he will neither change his behavior nor leave the organization, then the manager needs to let him go. Though it may still be somewhat painful, the manager will be able to act with relatively little guilt, knowing that he did everything possible to achieve a better outcome. That will go a long way toward helping employees feel

good about the situation, and reduce the possibility of lawsuits that come about when a difficult employee is surprised.

But perhaps the greatest outcome of choosing the direct approach will be the message it sends to the rest of the organization: we have standards of behavior, those standards have consequences, and your leader has the courage to enforce those consequences. That is something that any leader, in any organization, in any era, should be able to appreciate.

⏤ OCTOBER 2010

Rethinking Innovation

Perhaps the most popular—and misunderstood—term of the first decade of the new millennium is 'innovation.' A new stack of books and articles is produced every year asserting the critical importance of innovation for organizations that want to survive, especially during these challenging times. And to a large extent, I agree with that assertion. Unfortunately, most organizations in search of innovation seem to be generating as much cynicism as they are new thinking.

The problem isn't so much that we're over-stating the importance of innovation; it's more about what so many leaders are doing with it. Too many of them are exhorting all of their employees to be more innovative, providing classes and workshops designed to teach everyone how to think outside the box. They're also doing their best to include innovation on a list of core values, emblazoning the word on annual reports and hallway posters, hoping that this will inspire people to come up with new ideas that will revolutionize the long-term strategic and financial prospects of the company.

Even well-intentioned and dedicated employees are bound to respond cynically to these efforts, frustrated by what they see as hypocrisy. They just don't perceive a genuine eagerness among leaders to embrace the new ideas of rank-and-file employees, and they're mostly accurate in that perception. For all the talk about innovation, most executives don't really like the prospect of their people generating new ways to do things, hoping instead that they'll simply do what they're being asked to do in the most enthusiastic, professional way possible. And so it is no surprise when they get pounded for preaching innovation without really valuing it.

What should leaders do? Be more open to new ideas from employees? Probably not. Better yet, they should stop over-hyping innovation to the masses and come to the realization that only a limited number of people in any company really needs to be innovative.

As heretical as that may seem to those who want to believe that "innovation is everyone's business!", consider that even the most innovative and creative organizations need far more people to be dutiful, enthusiastic and consistent in their work than innovative or creative.

Think about a movie set. For every writer or director or actor on the payroll, there are hoards of people who have to be technically proficient, consistent, patient and disciplined in their responsibilities. If they innovate, the project turns to chaos.

And the most creative restaurant requires the work of a single chef to design a fabulous menu, and dozens of cooks and waitresses and waiters and dishwashers who will do their job with commitment, consistency and dutifulness. If the cooks innovate, consistency is gone and customers can't rely on what they're going to get. Even a high tech company, regardless of what they say, doesn't want or need its finance department or sales staff to be truly innovative.

What should leaders demand of their people, if not innovation? How about a combination of interpersonal creativity and autonomy? We need our employees to take complete responsibility to do their jobs and satisfy customers in the most effective and charismatic way possible, but within the bounds of sound business principles. For those who say, "well, that's what we mean when we use the word 'innovation'," you need to realize that it's not what your employees are hearing.

The combination of creativity and autonomy is something that thrives in great companies. The world's best airlines (e.g. Southwest), quick-service restaurants companies (e.g. Chick-fil-A), department stores (e.g. Nordstrom) and entrepreneurial businesses excel in it. Their employees are passionate and committed and take complete responsibility for their work, consistently turning customers into loyal fans. Sure, they're encouraged to share their ideas about new ways to work, but most of what they are known for is being great at what has already been defined as the product or service that their company offers. And most leaders I know would take that any day, even before innovation

Now that I've discouraged the wholesale application of innovation within a company, I'd like to backtrack a little. There is one group of people in an organization that has to exercise the capacity for innovation, regardless of their functional area. That group is the leadership team. Those who are chartered with overseeing a company's various departments from the top are the keepers of innovation. They are ultimately responsible for determining the boundaries of change that are

acceptable, and perhaps most important of all, identifying the handful of others within their departments who have the invitation and freedom to innovate.

So, if you're a leader, the next time you think about giving a speech or sending out an e-mail calling for your people to innovate, consider being more specific about what you really want from them. And if you really believe that your organization isn't innovative enough, focus your efforts first on the people at the top.

— AUGUST 2010

Undercover Boss

As we move into the season of television re-runs, I thought I might share a thought I had about a TV show that I've watched recently.

The truth is, I don't watch a lot of television. That's probably due in equal parts to my busy schedule these days and my distaste for most of what I see coming out of Hollywood. I hope that doesn't make me sound like a grumpy old man. In any case, when it comes to knowing what is happening on *Lost* or *24* or *American Idol*, I will admit that I'm woefully uninformed.

However, enough people encouraged me to watch the relatively new show *Undercover Boss* that I finally took the time to view a few episodes. And while I realize that it is designed for entertainment purposes and not as a training tool for leaders, I must admit that I was still disappointed in what I saw.

Before I get into my reasons for that, I should probably explain the basic premise of the show, especially for those who haven't seen it. Essentially, in each episode a CEO or senior executive anonymously takes a front line position within his or her organization, usually in some sort of blue collar job. Of the episodes I've seen, those jobs included riding in a garbage truck, working as a clerk at a convenience store, driving a delivery van and working on the assembly line in a bakery.

Now, this is a terrific concept. In theory, the show would seem to be a great way to give viewers a glimpse of the realities of corporate America, and more importantly, to encourage leaders to rethink how well they know what's happening in their organizations. In reality, the show is painful. Here's why.

First, the way the show is produced and edited is overwrought and misleading. Beyond the cheesy opening that sounds more like the intro to a professional wrestling match than a documentary, I find it maddening how the producers insert dramatic music and suggestive camera shots to add artificial tension to meetings and other situations that are otherwise fairly undramatic. I suppose what really bugs me is the possibility that viewers who have never worked in corporate

America might come to believe that business really does resemble a Donald Trump reality TV show. It doesn't.

But more than the editing, I don't like the way the 'bosses' have to act when they are on camera. It's clear to me that they are not saying what they're really thinking, but instead are trying to manage the perceptions of a television audience. And though I can't blame them for doing so given the potential for positive or negative PR, the impact is nonetheless shmarmy.

You see, in all the episodes I saw, the undercover executive, who was woefully undertrained for the lower level job he was taking on, came to an emotional realization that he was out of touch with what was really going on in the organization. As a result, he gained a profound new appreciation for the challenges and travails of the employees down in the trenches. And while that in itself would seem like a good thing, the behavior of the executives featured-lots of hugs and apologies-made me feel like I was watching an episode of Celebrity Rehab instead of a documentary on organizational life. Again, I realize that's the nature of TV, but it was painful nonetheless.

What I'd prefer to see is someone with real business experience interviewing the executives after each episode and really probing them about how they spend their time and why they don't understand what is happening in the organizations they lead. And I'd want to hear the executives give us their unfiltered comments about their own challenges and why solutions can't quite be captured in a one-hour made-for-TV program. Finally, I'd love to see someone do follow-up interviews three months later to see how the executives made changes based on what they learned.

But I suppose that wouldn't make for great television, so producers wouldn't go for it. Unless, of course, the CEOs then sang show tunes or danced the samba and then let their employees harshly grade their performances. Now that would be must-see TV.

Having said all that, there is a valuable lesson to be learned from *Undercover Boss*. I think all leaders should spend time on the front lines of their companies, on a regular basis and without TV cameras and background music, reminding themselves what the world looks like from the vantage point of employees and customers. In addition to the obvious benefits of staying informed,

it is a wonderful way to keep executives humble and remind them about the ultimate purpose of leadership, which is service.

— JUNE 2010

What Clients Really Want

When I graduated from college and became a management consultant, one of the first things I was taught was how to answer questions from clients without giving away my age or lack of business experience. "Instead of admitting that you graduated from college last spring, just say that it's been a while since you were in school." The underlying message was that we needed to portray ourselves as having more knowledge and experience than we actually did.

This carried over into our work. When we went to clients, we were taught to have done plenty of research and to have formulated a recommendation, one that was backed up by solid data and analysis. We were expected to portray ourselves as being smart (and frankly, that meant smarter than the clients), and advised to do nothing that might demonstrate a lack of confidence or authority.

As a result, many of my colleagues, including me, came to dislike our jobs. And to be fair, it didn't feel like our clients liked us much either. But that was the world of consulting, and unfortunately, in many places, it still is.

When I left that job and joined a 'real' company, I became a client myself, bringing in consultants to do projects for my organization. I suppose that it was somewhere during that time that I developed my current approach to consulting, one that we've been using in my firm for the past dozen years. It's called naked consulting and, yes, it's as intriguing as it sounds.

The essence of naked consulting is that clients are more interested in candor, humility and transparency than they are in confidence, authority and perfection. That's not to say that competence is irrelevant; clients need to know that we have the knowledge and experience to help them. But once we've reached that level, the best way to differentiate ourselves from competition—not to mention help a client implement the ideas we're recommending to them—is to be vulnerable with them.

Vulnerability is the opposite of, well, invulnerability. It's about honesty and authenticity. And it's about overcoming the understandable fears that cause us to say and do things that hurt our relationships with clients. Those include the fear of losing our clients' business, the fear of being embarrassed or looking stupid in front of clients, and the fear of putting ourselves in a position of inferiority with our clients. I say these fears are understandable because no one wants to lose business, look stupid or feel inferior. Ironically, it is only by facing and overcoming those fears, and getting comfortable being naked, that we can earn the kind of trust that creates loyalty with clients.

What does being naked look like in practice? Naked consultants confront clients (kindly) with difficult information and perspectives, even if the client might not like hearing it. They also admit their weaknesses and willingly acknowledge their mistakes. Naked consultants also ask potentially dumb questions, and make potentially dumb suggestions, because if asking those questions or suggestions might help their clients, then it is worth doing.

Even before landing a client, a naked consultant will demonstrate vulnerability and take risks. They will give away their best ideas and start consulting to the prospective client during a sales call. In fact, they'll do no real selling at all, foregoing that activity in order to find a way to help a potential client even if they never actually become a real, paying one.

If all this sounds a little counterintuitive, even crazy, that's because it is, at least to many consultants and service providers. It puts them in a position of potential weakness and exposure, and increases the possibility that they'll be taken advantage of. But to clients, that weakness and exposure is seen as honesty, generosity, and a demonstration of our humanity. And no matter how hard we may try to convince ourselves that clients expect us to be superhuman, in reality what they want more than anything else is for us to be, yes, simply human.

Which is what makes naked consulting so ironic, and difficult. In order to demonstrate our humanity, to do what will endear us to clients like nothing else, we have to do something

that is unnatural for most of us to do. Here's hoping that we can all find the courage to be unnaturally human.

— FEBRUARY 2010

 The content from this article was based on Pat's book, *Getting Naked*. For more information about the book, the model and free tools, please visit www.tablegroup.com.

The Corporate Flu Season

This has been a big year for the flu, and my family was certainly not spared from it. It was a long and painful Fall in our house, though we seem to be largely recovered, thank God.

Now, if you're anything like me, when you get sick you find yourself yearning desperately to be healthy again. You pledge that when you get better you're really going to appreciate your health, not take it for granted. And if you're anything like me, when you do get better, you too easily forget how you felt when you were ill and eventually start doing the same things—eating poorly, working too hard, staying up too late at night, forgetting to take vitamins—that make you susceptible to catching the next flu bug that comes around.

I think the same thing happens in our companies: whether our sickness is an extended decrease in demand for our products or we're struggling to fight off a serious competitive threat. As leaders, we understandably get desperate to get our business healthy again, and just when we start to worry that maybe it will never improve, the 'flu' runs its course, things finally start to get better, and we feel a sense of relief.

But rather than appreciate our new situation, we are often all too happy to put the problem behind us, causing us to lose a sense of gratitude for having lived through it. Perhaps, in a state of minor delusion, we congratulate ourselves for solving the problem, and even develop a measure of arrogance about the whole thing. Not only does this make us more susceptible to having those problems again in the future, it prevents us from seeing the valuable lessons we can learn during the process of being not well.

Well, I'd say that our economy is currently in the middle of a very long and very painful flu season, and virtually every organization is in some way infected. Our symptoms can be found in our financial performance, our strategic uncertainty, our sagging morale. As painful as this is and as much as we want it to be over, it is actually a good time to take a long look at the situation we're in and ask ourselves a few important questions. What did we do to make us susceptible to this?

How could we have diminished our symptoms had we known the flu was coming? What will we do differently once this passes?

The key to doing this is two-fold. First, we have to resist the temptation to lament the problem. Wasting time cursing the situation only keeps us from seeing the underlying lessons. Second, we have to avoid the tendency to simply work more, spin faster and grind harder, because that is just a recipe for getting sicker. Instead, we have to slow down, come to gentle terms with the reality of our situation, and look for opportunities to change the way we approach our work. That might mean new products and services, a different strategy, better use of partners, or some other change that we wouldn't have considered if we had never caught the flu in the first place. Whatever it is, by changing our perspective from self-pity to self-improvement, we'll actually hasten our recovery.

Now I realize that this sounds somewhat clichéd and that it is a lot easier said than done. When revenue is down and the sales pipeline is looking a little dry, it's not easy to look on the bright side. But that's what makes great companies great: they do the things that are hard and simple.

So, as we prepare for the New Year, let's make a special effort to stop and count our blessings, even during this time of relative difficulty. And let's not forget that when all is said and done, this flu we're living through, as painful as it is, may make us more resilient to sickness in the future, and actually prove to be a blessing in disguise.

— DECEMBER 2009

The Enemy of Innovation and Creativity

Maybe it was just the kind of kid I was, but I'm guessing that most children are constantly reminded by adults to be more efficient. Maybe not exactly in those words. More likely it comes in the form of phrases like "don't be late", "use your time wisely", "don't waste money" or even "turn off the lights when you leave a room".

And while it's difficult to argue with a parent's or teacher's or coach's motivation for instilling these principles in the youngsters they're responsible for, there comes a time in life—especially in certain situations—when those very traits become problematic. One of those situations is the call to innovation or creativity.

I've become convinced that the only way to be really creative and innovative in life is to be joyfully inefficient. Again, maybe it's just my personality, but I'm guessing it applies to most of us whose jobs or lives involve dreaming up or improving on new ideas. And this makes sense. Asking someone to be both creative and efficient reminds me of that quote from Einstein: "You cannot simultaneously prevent and prepare for war." The two activities are fundamentally opposed to one another.

Efficiency requires that we subdue our passion and allow it to be constrained by principles of logic and convention. Innovation and creativity require us to toss aside logic and convention, even without the near-term promise of a payoff. Embracing both at the same time seems to me to be a recipe for stress, dissonance and mediocrity, and yet, that is exactly what so many organizations—or better yet—leaders, do.

They exhort their employees to utilize their resources wisely and to avoid waste and redundancy, which makes perfect sense. They also exhort them to be ever-vigilant about finding new and better products or processes, which also makes sense. And yet, combining these two perfectly sensible exhortations makes no sense at all, and only encourages rational, responsible people to find a middle ground, something that is decidedly neither efficient nor innovative.

So what are leaders, who want both, to do? First, choose their poison; decide which of these two characteristics are truly more important and live with the consequences. And, when you simply have to have both, create skunkworks efforts which allow a small group of people to be joyfully inefficient. No guilt. No confusion. No hesitation. And keep them largely separate from their efficient peers, at least until they've developed their ideas and are ready to share them.

But whatever you do, don't chide creative, innovative people for their inefficiency. And try to avoid throwing faint praise and backhanded compliments at them (e.g. "I guess you creative types just aren't capable of hitting a deadline or staying on budget"). Few people have the self-esteem and courage to continue being inefficient when others are calling them out as being flaky, irresponsible and unreasonable. If we're serious about innovation, we have to celebrate—yes, celebrate—the inefficiency of the people who we rely on for new ideas, even if it means they are late for meetings, they waste a little time or money and they leave the lights on when they go home.

— OCTOBER 2009

Diversity's Missing Ingredient

When it comes to tapping into the competitive advantage of diversity, few companies succeed. Yesterday I was reminded why.

Our firm was having a meeting to discuss important elements of our strategy and marketing efforts, when something really great happened—we got into an argument. Not a disagreement. A loud, contentious, uncomfortable and passionate argument.

On one side of the battle was a pair of our team members who were arguing their point based on a very accurate and literal interpretation of something we had decided months earlier. On the other side was a group of team members that was even more loudly making their point (probably because I was a member of that group and I'm Italian and Irish) based on a more theoretical interpretation of that past decision.

For a few minutes, our debate sounded more like a brawl, with team members calling each other out for their intellectual biases and blind spots. Fortunately, because there is a great deal of trust on our team, our argument never came anywhere close to personal or mean-spirited attacks, though an outsider who didn't know us certainly would have thought it did.

When the melee was over and we had arrived at a decision, a couple of things occurred to me. First, the conflict we had engaged in—as uncomfortable as it felt at the time—was a wonderful thing, because it allowed us to get closer to the truth, which often lies somewhere between two divergent points of view (though this was not a new revelation for me, I am amazed at how much I still need reminders). Second, those divergent points of view were based, not on randomness, but on the diverse personality profiles of the people on either side; one side was comprised of our more rational and data-driven team members while the other represented our more emotional, intuition-dependent people

Which brings me back to the power of diversity, and the reason why it remains so misunderstood and under-exploited in most organizations: it requires conflict.

The practical advantage of diversity boils down to this: a group of people with different perspectives usually makes better decisions and finds more creative solutions than those who have largely similar views, backgrounds and skill sets. This is true for all teams, whether they're running a corporation, a church, a school or a movie studio. However, when a team cannot productively engage in conflict, not only does that diversity remain untapped, it becomes a competitive disadvantage.

That's because when team members with divergent points of view cannot openly and passionately advocate their positions, the team will not be able to properly understand and incorporate those ideas into a final decision. Instead, they will frustratingly agree to compromise, walking away dissatisfied with the outcome and resentful of their team members who they still don't understand.

This is the norm in virtually every organization where I've worked or consulted. And that's because when we talk about diversity, the emphasis is usually on acceptance and tolerance and "getting along." All of which, of course, are good things. The problem surfaces when those qualities prevent people from challenging one another's points of view out of fear of being labeled close-minded or intolerant.

And so the key to making diversity work is to teach people first how to appreciate one another's differences, and then how to challenge them in the context of pursuing the best possible outcome. When a company can do that, it will transform diversity from a slogan to a real competitive advantage.

— JUNE 2009

Mission or Performance: The False Dilemma

During a recent plane ride, I found myself sitting next to a former colleague from my first job as a management consultant. Actually, he was the leader of the consulting firm where I worked, but he's now running a different consulting firm that focuses on non-profits.

After having the inevitable conversation about the differences between consulting to for-profits and not-for-profits (I'll call them FPs and NFPs), a question occurred to me: why do we make such a distinction between the two? The only real distinction between them is a financial/legal one. Why is one of our primary delineations between organizations based on whether or not they pay taxes and are allowed to distribute excess capital to employees and shareholders?

Of course, anyone who has worked in or consulted to NFPs will tell you that the differences between FPs and NFPs is much greater than taxes and capital distribution, that it involves culture, attitude, accountability, strategy and a host of other things.

And that's the thing; I don't know that it should. Perhaps we've just allowed organizations on both sides of the profit aisle to choose their own areas of mediocrity and lower standards.

So many NFPs (but not all of them) are allowed to accept lower levels of accountability and productivity and rigor around ROI than their FP counterparts. What is the rationale? Since they rely on volunteers and don't pay as much to their staff members, they can't expect us much.

And so many FPs (but again, not all of them) feel no need to tap into the passions and idealism of their employees, and give them a sense of mission. Why? Because their purpose is to maximize compensation for investors, and everything else is just window dressing.

Of course, this is ridiculous, and only makes sense if we see employees as either puppies or robots, incapable of simultaneously embracing two distinct motivations and outlooks. The fact is, all of us are part puppy and part robot. We want to be motivated by something meaningful, and we want ourselves, and others, to be held accountable for their performance and the value they produce.

So perhaps leaders need to stop thinking of their organizations as FPs and NFPs and start using a more meaningful and actionable criteria for categorization.

Is your organization going to be a mission-driven one (an MD), or a performance-driven one (a PD)?

Of course, the greatest leaders will choose both. They will inspire their employees around something more meaningful than simply profit, and they'll drive them to standards of measurable performance regardless of whether or not the CFO has to pay taxes at the end of the year or how they distribute excess capital. They'll choose to make their organizations MDPDs. Now there's a catchy four letter acronym.

— APRIL 2009

Rediscovering Work

Sometimes when we're in the midst of a major event or a crisis, we don't notice big changes that are happening around us. And then, when things settle down and we get up off the floor, we look around and notice that some parts of life have fundamentally shifted. I think that is what's going on right now in the way people see employment.

When I graduated from college and started looking for a job a little over twenty years ago, there seemed to be a new attitude emerging—one that had probably been slowly taking shape for twenty years before that—about the importance of finding deep meaning and fulfillment in a job. Gone were the days of simply looking for a secure job in a stable industry. The new movement encouraged young people to find their true passions, be unconventional, and blaze their own trails.

I have to admit that I was a big proponent—and still am—of helping people discover their talents and gifts and find an outlet for them in work is one of my favorite hobbies. I'll also admit that I assumed that this new ascent up Maslow's hierarchy of needs would never be reversed. But, given the fundamental changes we're seeing in the global economy, we may just be sliding back down Maslow's pyramid a little, and maybe even staying there for a while. In other words, I think we're going to start having lower expectations about finding the perfect, meaningful and custom-fitted job, and developing a new kind of appreciation for the old notion of work.

Now, don't get me wrong. I'm not happy about this. The thought of fewer people going to work with a sense of idealism and passion and fulfillment is a little disheartening to me. (I even wrote a book about it.) However, I believe some hidden blessings may come out of all this.

For one, this emphasis on finding a perfect job has created something of a sense of guilt or disappointment for so many people who, because of economic or educational limitations, weren't in a position to land their dream job. They never became a roller-coaster architect or an author of children's books or a rocket scientist. Instead, they did the best they could to find a relatively interesting job in a field that would allow them to pay the bills. Given everything that's happening today, they're going to be feeling better about what they're doing, and happier than ever to simply be working. That's a good thing.

And then there are the people who were industrious and fortunate enough to find one of those cool jobs, but who experienced their own disappointment when they came to the inevitable realization that designing roller coasters and writing books and building rockets didn't turn out to be the party they expected it to be, and that a rewarding career is not the answer to all of life's problems. The fact is, even rock stars and advertising executives and fashion designers experience the drudgery of work, not unlike bank tellers and plumbers and retail clerks; they just feel worse about it because they didn't expect their work to become, well, work. Now they too can find a little relief and reset their expectations about the reality of having a job.

Finally, and most importantly, this shift away from needing a perfect job might just bring about a new appreciation for the simple gift that is work. This is something that my parents' generation seemed to understand better than mine. To be gainfully employed, to labor with integrity in any way for the good of customers or co-workers or family, really can be its own reward. That is making sense to me now more than it has at any time in my career.

Let's hope and pray that the job situation turns around soon so we can put this theory to the test.

— MARCH 2009

Virtual Teams

When I speak to audiences about teamwork, one of the most frequently asked questions I get has to do with managing groups of people who are geographically dispersed, a.k.a. virtual teams. This surprises me a little because the topic, as well as the solution for addressing it, is certainly not very sexy. But with so many teams these days comprised of members living in different time zones and countries and continents, and with travel budgets likely to shrink for the foreseeable future, there probably has never been a greater need for people who don't see each other very often to figure out how to work better together. The key is simply about avoiding three mistakes.

The first mistake that virtual teams make is underestimating the challenges of being dispersed. Because e-mail and voicemail and texting and instant messaging have become so second nature, we too often assume that a team member's physical location makes little difference in the effectiveness of the team. This, of course, makes no sense.

After all, no family would say "well, dad lives in New York, mom lives in San Francisco and the kids are spread around the country, but thanks to my iPhone and computer, it's no different than living under the same roof." The simple but often overlooked truth is that without the daily interaction of breakfast or dinner or homework or late night conversations or doing the dishes, a family can't possibly develop and maintain the strength that it needs to thrive during good times and survive during challenging ones. The same is true for teams who have no incidental conversations in the hallway or at lunch, or in the elevator, for that matter.

Once a team understands the disadvantage of not being co-located, then it will be more likely to take on the next mistake that virtual teams make: wasting the precious time that they do spend together.

Too many virtual teams utilize their quarterly or monthly in-person sessions engaging in social activities, somehow believing that this is how the team will bond. While social time is okay, if there is not a focused and organized attempt to build relationships in the context of the work that needs to be done, then the team will only improve its collective golf scores, or worse yet, its tolerance for alcohol. On the other side of the equation, too many teams go the other way, spending their sparse time together doing detailed operations reviews and addressing overly tactical matters, which is almost as unproductive as golfing. The perfect storm occurs when teams split their time between irrelevant socializing and mind-numbing detail, resulting almost inevitably in everyone coming to dread another useless trip to corporate.

What team members really need to do when they are face-to-face is develop their relationships by getting to know one another's strengths and weaknesses, not in a touchy-feely way, but in the context of the goals of the business. And they need to establish clear alignment around the bigger picture issues like the team's core purpose, values, strategic anchors and top priorities. Wasting time in the weeds wrestling with detailed ops issues is fruitless and frustrating when teams are not on the same page relating to these bigger issues. Strong relationships are critical to getting on the same page because it allows the team to debate issues passionately and productively, which increases the likelihood that everyone will buy-in.

Buy-in is especially important for virtual team members, because when they get back to their offices, they will need to work with a high degree of confidence that their peers will do what they agreed to do for the good of the team. That is hard enough when those peers sit in the cube or office across the hall and have plenty of in-person meetings on a regular basis. When they're in different cities, it is much more difficult, which brings us to mistake number three.

The last mistake that virtual teams make is failing to master an event that is one of the most loathed and underestimated of all corporate activities: the dreaded conference call. Yes, even in this age of improved video-conferencing, there is simply no good, reliable and affordable everyday substitute for the speaker phone when it comes to working with remote colleagues. Unfortunately, just as we've done with regular meetings, we've come to believe that conference calls are inherently boring and unchangeable, a sort of corporate penance. So we accept agenda items that are neither compelling or critical, and we make an unspoken deal with each other: "as long as you let me check my e-mail and balance my check-book and play spider solitaire and do busy work—all with the mute button on—I'll keep coming to these meetings and offering my perfunctory input to let everyone know I'm still awake."

What teams have to do—and I told you up front that this is simple and unsexy—is make a serious commitment to one another that they will maintain a high standard of behavior during conference calls, even higher than they would for an in-person meeting. That will mean eliminating outside interruptions, avoiding distractions, foregoing the use of the mute button, and indicating agreement or disagreement verbally to avoid passive approvals born out of misinterpreted silence.

Of course, all of this starts with the building of strong relationships, and the only way our teams are going to be willing to dedicate the time and energy to do that is if we understand the disadvantage of being virtual. If we can't do that, we should probably just get used to more golf, more spider solitaire, and more time, energy and money wasted during trips to corporate.

— FEBRUARY 2009

 The content from this article was based on Pat's book, *The Five Dysfunctions of a Team*. For more on the book, the model and free tools, please visit www.tablegroup.com.

The "Down Economy" Bandwagon

It seems like we've been preparing for this current recession for the past two or three years, constantly predicting it and staving it off as long as we could, all the while listening to the media tell us that it was just around the corner. And now that it is here—and it is here—we're witnessing a new media-inspired cottage industry building up around the "down economy" and the bad times that are upon us and that lie ahead.

Every news story seems to have the addendum "in a bad economy" attached to it. I suspect that soon there will be a new "Recession Barbie" doll on toy store shelves, complete with a frown on her face and a copy of the job listings from the newspaper in her hands.

Well, so far I've resisted jumping onto the "down economy" bandwagon, not wanting to contribute to any self-fulfilling prophecy or culture of victimization that can make a bad situation worse. But after numerous requests, I've agreed to share my own perspectives about how leaders can survive and even thrive during difficult times.

The first thing we have to do is ask ourselves a fundamental question: do we believe things will get better? If we don't, if we believe this is the definitive end to any upside in the economy and that it's all downhill from here, then I'm afraid I have no good advice. Aside from moving somewhere that does have an economic upside.

But most of us would admit that this, too, will rebound. Maybe not the same way it has in the past. After all, there are some fundamental problems that we haven't yet faced. But even in the absence of that, there is a good chance that we will experience an economic upturn sometime in the not-too-too-distant future. And if that is the case, our call to action is clear: use this time to invest in your organization's future, especially when the investment is not a financial one.

The best place for an investment right now is in the general health of an organization. I'm talking mostly about improving the functioning of the executive team, and their clarification of and recommitment to the organization's values and purpose. Doing this will require a little time and energy, but very little money. And it will yield significant returns now, and even more when the economy rebounds. How?

A wise executive team will take this opportunity during slow times to build greater trust and behavioral cohesiveness. This will benefit the organization by minimizing politics and infighting, that are common during difficult times, and it will allow the team to make better decisions about which programs and employees need to be retained and which shouldn't. All of this will allow the organization to emerge stronger than ever when the economy turns around, and with a meaningful advantage over competitors.

That's because most of those competitors will probably flail during down times, frantically searching for a tactical way to swim upstream and defy the current, leading to even more frustration and angst than is necessary. In the end they'll simply be more weary and scarred and unprepared.

Of course, like so much of the advice that people are repositioning these days for a "down economy", none of this is really new. Even during good times leaders should be investing in the health of their teams. But with so many shiny opportunities in front of them, they often fail to slow down and do what it is best for the long term. Now that there are fewer and fewer of those shiny opportunities, there is no good excuse. And that may turn out to be a good thing.

— JANUARY 2009

 For more information on how to build a healthy organization, please visit www.tablegroup.com.

CEO Pay

For some reason, I haven't directly addressed this topic in any of my writings over the years. It's not because I'm afraid to or that I find it uninteresting. I think it has more to do with having such mixed feelings.

On the one hand, I think the amount of money paid to so many high profile chief executives is bizarrely and tragically excessive. But my take on that excess is different than most. See, I honestly believe that the ridiculous salaries and compensation some CEOs receive is a function of pride more than greed.

I may be naïve, but I just cannot fathom how someone who already has five homes and enough money socked away to put seventy five kids through college can really want more. What is it that they need the money for? Anyone with that much of it must have already come to the realization that it can't make them happy. That's why I honestly believe that the pursuit of higher salaries, bigger bonuses, more lucrative stock options and fluffier golden parachutes is more about keeping up with the Jones' than it is about money. CEOs know what their peers earn, and they want to compare favorably for the sake of their egos more than their bank accounts.

Regardless of the reason, the excessive payouts to executives—especially to the ones who fail—is just plain wrong.

On the other hand, I'm not in favor of addressing the problem through regulation and government involvement. Most fiscal matters the government involves itself in get worse, not better, and letting bureaucrats and politicians tamper with a free-market economy feels like a very bad idea to me.

And for those executives who lead their organizations to financial success, a healthy reward for their work can be justified. Running a company is a demanding and lonely job, and success should be rewarded. However, failure should not be, and far too much of the compensation awarded to chief executives is guaranteed and not tied to performance.

So what is our recourse?

Because of my belief that pride is at the heart of this problem, I think the solution must focus on reintroducing a healthy sense of shame—that's right—shame, to the marketplace. CEOs should be made publically accountable for the amount of money they make, and the men and women who serve on the boards that approve their compensation packages should share in that accountability. What would that look like?

First, the CEOs of publically traded companies should have their compensation packages made public. Yes, I realize that those packages are already available to anyone who takes a few minutes on the internet to look for it. But I'm thinking of something easier and more naked.

Perhaps, CEOs should have to explain their pay to their employees twice a year, justifying the money they make in light of their contribution to company success. And I'm not thinking of a formal board meeting where an employee would have to risk his or her hide to make a statement, but rather an on-line town hall with video coverage in which employees can anonymously and respectfully demand an explanation.

And maybe those same CEOs should be pressured to include their salary and compensation package at the bottom of their e-mail messages. For instance:

Fred Johnson
CEO, XYZ Corporation
Phone: 212-555-1212 e-mail: fred@xyz.com
Compensation: $2.5 million salary, 12 million stock options, $1 million guaranteed bonus

And wouldn't it be interesting if whenever a CEO receives a ridiculous bonus after a dismal year, or a golden parachute as a reward for running a company into the ground, he or she should be forced to sit in the lobby of the company's building for two weeks and endure the reaction of employees?

Finally, more industry analysts and television commentators should ask CEOs questions about their compensation. Because just knowing that they might have to publicly explain why they make so much money would give executives a reason to pause and reconsider if they would rather be known among their peers as getting the most lucrative deal or held in high esteem by employees, customers and shareholders for being responsible and humble.

But whatever we do—and I mean this—let's do it with love and charity. If we simply demonize CEOs and create an 'Us vs. Them' atmosphere, we only contribute to the animosity and division that probably enabled this situation to come about in the first place. Even when we correct and hold people accountable for changing their ways, we must do it out of love.

— DECEMBER 2008

Right-sizing Your Team

Right-sizing has to be one of the more detested words in modern business language, mostly because the use of it often indicates a lack of courage. Rather than come right out and say 'lay-off' or 'firing,' too many leaders announce that they are going to right-size their organization, as though this will somehow change the reality of what they are about to do, which is eliminate jobs and let employees go.

Of course, eliminating jobs and laying people off is a reality of business and no one can fault a leader who has to make those difficult decisions as long as they do it with appropriate discernment and gravity. What is ironic to me is how often executives fail to step up to the plate when it is time to do what the term right-sizing actually means, particularly when it comes to dealing with their leadership team.

So many executive teams I deal with are simply too big. Whether they have eleven or fourteen or eighteen members, they become gangly and cumbersome, making it impossible to be nimble and responsive in their responsibilities to steer their organization through rough waters, or even relatively calm ones.

So what is the right size for a leadership team? Somewhere between three and eight. Why? Because groups larger than this almost always struggle to effectively use the two kinds of communication that are required of any organization.

Chris Argyris, a professor at Harvard, came up with the idea years ago that people need to engage in both 'advocacy' and 'inquiry' in order to communicate effectively. Advocacy amounts to stating an opinion or an idea, while inquiry is the act of asking questions or seeking clarity about someone else's opinion or idea. Frankly, one part advocacy and two parts inquiry is a mix I like to see on teams.

However, when there are too many people at the table, inquiry drops off dramatically, mostly because people realize that they're not going to get many opportunities to speak so they weigh in with their opinion while they have the chance. Like a member of congress or the United Nations, they aren't going to waste their precious time at the pulpit to exploring the merits of a colleague's proposal. Where is the glory in that?

But when the team is smaller, two things happen. First, trust can be exponentially stronger. That is simply a matter of physics. Second, team members know that they'll have plenty of time to make their ideas heard, even if they do more inquiry than advocacy. This leads to significantly better and faster decisions. That's worth repeating. Better AND faster. Those large teams I referred to before often take three times longer to arrive at decisions that prove to be much poorer, often the result of a grope for consensus.

So, how does a leader go about right-sizing a team?

First, understand the reason for having such a large team in the first place. Too often, they put people on the team as a reward, or to placate them for another unrelated issue. "I'll put Fred on the executive committee. Then he won't feel so bad about having part of his organization taken away." Or maybe, "the merger has been painful for everyone. I'll just have two VPs of sales at the meeting. No need to alienate anyone right now." Along the same lines but for somewhat different reasons, they fall for the inclusivity plea, trying to demonstrate to the organization that they are open to many different opinions and that they value everyone's input.

Once a leader has come to terms with why the team has grown so large, it becomes time to right-size the team. The key to doing this is to avoid the band-aid approach, which involves painfully choosing people to take off the team, one at a time. A better method is to create a new team, starting from scratch. That means if you have twelve people on the team, rather than winnowing it down to ten or nine, try forming a real executive team with just four or five. Add one or two more from there if necessary, and unapologetically explain to the old team why the new one is necessary, and why you've formed it the way you did.

You can keep the old team intact for other purposes, like communication and development, but not for making the regular decisions that must be made quickly and with the right mix of debate and decisiveness.

One of the things you'll learn is that the people who are not on the new team will probably thank you. In many cases, they see and experience the dysfunction of too many members, and while there may be a temporary sting at not being on the new one, any good executive will be mature enough to see the benefits to the organization overall. And if they aren't mature enough to do that, you probably shouldn't have had them on the team in the first place.

— NOVEMBER 2008

Not Everyone Should Lead

I always find it interesting—or maybe troubling—when people encourage everyone to go out and vote on election day. Don't get me wrong; I'm an ardent fan of democracy. I just don't think it's a good idea for people to vote unless they've taken the time to understand the issues and make informed decisions. It would be far better, in my opinion, if those who are too busy or disinterested to stay abreast of the issues exercised restraint on election day. I think that makes perfect sense, and yet is often viewed as politically or socially incorrect.

Well, I have a similar attitude about leadership. Whenever I hear someone encourage all young people to become leaders, or better yet, when I hear a young person say glibly that he or she wants to be a leader someday, I feel compelled to ask the question "why?"

If the answer is "because I want to make a difference" or "I want to change the world," I get a little skeptical and have to ask a follow-up question: "Why and in what way do you want to change the world?" If they struggle to answer that question, I discourage them from becoming a leader.

Why? Because a leader who doesn't know why he or she wants to lead is almost always motivated by self-interest. Whether that manifests itself in terms of fame or money or power, it is a very dangerous thing.

True leadership, the kind that results in the greater good, requires a level of selflessness and vision that most people simply don't have. We forget the loneliness and sacrifice and great personal risk that George Washington and Abraham Lincoln endured during their times, and that the personal benefits they received for their sacrifices were minimal, if not non-existent. But that is what was—and is—required of any truly great leader, which explains why leadership is a rare trait in society, and always has been.

When people without selflessness become leaders, they often end up exploiting people and leaving them worse off. As long as they escape relatively unscathed, they feel that they have succeeded. And this is not limited to CEOs of big companies or members of Congress, though those cases are both more public and potentially harmful. It applies to small business owners, little league coaches, school principals and mid-level managers as well.

Perhaps that's why society has become so cynical about leaders, especially in the world of politics and, more recently, big business. People have come to expect—even accept—that their leaders are motivated by fame and fortune more than real service. Which is a shame because we are starting to get cynical as a society. As a result, the wrong people are being drawn into positions of leadership for all the wrong reasons.

So what is the solution? Like so many other aspects of life, it is both simple and difficult. First, we have to stop hiring, appointing and electing people who are ego-driven. That requires a level of discretion and vigilance on the part of CEOs, hiring managers, boards of directors, and yes, even voters. Of course, that means we also have to work hard to discern why a person is truly motivated to seek a position of leadership, and be wary of anyone who lacks humility, maturity and selflessness.

When it comes to elected office, this will require voters to pay close attention to the candidates who plea for their support. And if voters can't find the time and energy to do that, then the wisest decision they could make would be to exercise restraint and stay home on election day.

— OCTOBER 2008

The Financial Crisis

In the midst of the financial crisis going on in America these days, there is a natural tendency to search for a villain we can blame and move on with a sense of tidiness and moral certitude. Unfortunately, I don't think there is such a villain.

Sure, there's more than likely a good number of people who made serious mistakes out of carelessness or greed, and they will need to be held accountable for that. But the real culprit here, in my opinion, has nothing to do with economics or regulations or finance. It is about the desire of leaders to avoid interpersonal discomfort.

I realize that this doesn't sound very sexy, and certainly isn't going to make for a compelling television movie-of-the-week. It would be better if there were a group of sinister old men out there who sit around in three piece suits smoking stogies and laughing about how rich and powerful they are going to get stealing people's homes and investments. That would actually be easier because then we could track those guys down, throw them in jail, and achieve a measure of closure. But based on my experience consulting to CEOs and their teams over the past decade, I can say with a high degree of confidence that this just isn't the case.

The biggest cause of this and other crises is that most leaders operate under the assumption that they should never have to engage in discussions that are awkward, confrontational or career-limiting. As a result, they rarely have the kind of uncomfortable discussions that prevent people from doing stupid and harmful things. Instead, they are polite and guarded and collegial with one another, even when what is called for is passionate disagreement or even outrage.

This is a surprise to people who don't have a view into corporate America. They are usually shocked when I tell them that I rarely see people passionately argue with one another or take a strong, moral stand. What they don't realize is that the real world is nothing like what we see in movies where executives routinely pound their fists on the table and announce, "this is just plain wrong and I won't stand for it!"

Consider the current situation at various banks, some of which no longer exist. Plenty of intelligent and well-intentioned board members and executives must have known that something was wrong with granting a CEO a $20 million bonus in the event that he were fired. And even the least sophisticated executive had to have seen the potential problem with approving home loans to people who would not be able to afford them if and when interest rates changed. So why didn't they do something?

Because they looked around and saw other intelligent and well-intentioned people who weren't standing up on their chairs and objecting. And they figured that perhaps what was going on wasn't so bad after all, especially if so many other executives and banks and boards of directors were doing it. "Who am I to rain on this parade?"

To be fair, some of them probably made a quiet comment during a meeting, or more likely, mentioned something to another board member over lunch. But they weren't laying down on the railroad tracks and risking their compensation or their friendships or their reputation if no one else would. Of course, plenty of them will come out now and say they saw the problem all along, and they might even be able to convince enough people that they should be considered whistle blowers.

The fact is, too few people in life have the courage and clarity of thinking to stand up at the right time and say what needs to be said. And, that's what makes real leaders different. They are ready and willing to do what is unseemly, uncomfortable, and even personally risky for the sake of what is right.

So the lesson that comes from all of this, or at least one of the most important ones, has nothing to do with legislation or economic policy or oversight. It is a personal lesson that each of us can learn by honestly and humbly asking ourselves what we would have done had we been a board member or an executive at one of those companies that did something that seems so clearly wrong in hindsight. By considering that question, we will probably shift our emotional energy away from trying to find a legislative, economic or legal explanation for the mess we're in, and shine

the light on the behavioral one that really deserves the attention. Perhaps that will help us avoid the next crisis.

— SEPTEMBER 2008

Family Leadership

Most leaders I know have multiple jobs, even if they are only paid to do one of them. For instance, I am a leader of a small company, but I have leadership roles in my church, on my sons' soccer, baseball and basketball teams, and of course, in my family. However, when I think about all of those roles, and the constituencies who are impacted by them, I cannot help but conclude that my wife and kids have received short shrift when it comes to my leadership time and energy.

After all, I've spent hours and days and weeks thinking, reading and meeting about how to better run my company. I've worked with my team to identify our core values and to clarify our strategy. And I've worked to ensure that those values and strategies have been implemented consistently over time so that our firm can maximize its potential.

Within my church, I've spent many hours in long meetings developing plans to ensure that we're utilizing our resources in the best possible way. I regularly spend time preparing for each soccer or basketball practice I lead, and on multiple occasions I've attended two-day classes to make me a better soccer coach. I've even read a stack of books on soccer to give me an added edge.

Then there is my family, the most important organization in my life. How many books have I read about running an effective family? Zero. How many family management classes have I attended? None. And how many offsites have my wife and I had to improve the way we organize and lead our children? You know the answer.

As common as this is for many family leaders who also work in the 'real' world, it just doesn't make any sense. When we fail to be purposeful and proactive about the way we plan and run our home lives, our families become reactive, unfulfilled and frantic. And though we might not see a direct, short-term connection between this and downstream difficulties like divorce and childhood stress, it is hard to deny such a connection. Ongoing frustration and disillusionment among parents, even when it is minor, cannot help but have an impact on family members.

So what is a family to do? Something. Anything is better than sitting back and reacting to the next request or opportunity that comes along without any context. And that word—context—is key. It is what is missing from most frantic organizations, especially families.

Context provides leaders with a framework and a perspective that they need so that every opportunity that arises doesn't create a stressful dilemma. In the business world, a leader deciding to acquire a company or pursue a client or hire a candidate for a job, can often fall back on a clear set of values, strategic priorities or goals that will allow him to make consistently good decisions and retain a measure of sanity in the process.

The same is true at home. Without clear context, our lives become reactionary and stressful and often a guilt-driven act of daily survival rather than the joyful, intentional experience that it is meant to be. Should we sign Johnny up for lacrosse? Go on vacation with the Martins? Remodel our home like the Jones' or buy a summer cabin like the Johnsons? If there is nothing clear to fall back on, each decision will create unnecessary anxiety, not to mention months or years of potential regret.

So what exactly can families do to get some relief? They need to create a sense of context by answering a few simple questions, and then use those answers to guide their decisions. The questions have to do with a family's core values, strategic priorities and near-term goals. And once those answers are set, the family needs to keep them alive and use them on a daily, weekly and monthly basis. Of course, it's key to keep all of this simple and practical, and avoid overly structured or bureaucratic approaches, because families have even less time and tolerance for bureaucracy and protocol than companies do.

— AUGUST 2008

 The content from this article was based on Pat's book, *The Three Big Questions for a Frantic Family*. For more information on the book, model and free tools, please visit www.tablegroup.com.

The Underutilization of Moral Authority

One of the most common questions I get from readers of my books and audience members at my talks goes something like this: "What do I do if my manager is the problem on my team? I mean, I don't have control over him. How am I supposed to have any influence?" Sometimes the question isn't even about a manager, but about a peer or employee in another department within the organization.

I used to respond to those questions by encouraging people to try to focus on influencing their own department and maybe even accept their situation for what it is. While there is virtue in doing both of those things, I've recently come to the realization that there is an additional option-and a powerful one-that most of us are reticent to use, or perhaps unaware of. What I'm referring to is something I'll define as moral authority.

Moral authority, as I'm using it here, is simply the power we have to affect change by appealing to what is right and good. It exists above and beyond the formal power structure in any organization or society, and rests upon the idea that people generally want to do what is good and what is best. Most importantly, it is available to all of us with the courage and emotional intelligence to use it properly.

An example might be helpful.

Let's say my children fail to clean their room one day, and I announce that they have to go to bed a half hour early as punishment. If they believe my decision is unfair, they have a choice to make. They can tantrum, hoping that I'll somehow change my mind just to avoid the pain and suffering of listening to them complain. Or they can choose the more political route, and go to their mom and try to drive a rift between us. Or they can exercise their moral authority and calmly, directly explain that they didn't clean their room because they have a big school project due the next day, and they've been spending all of their time building an Egyptian pyramid out of sugar cubes.

Unless I'm a cold-hearted tyrant, there is a darn good chance that a reasonable explanation, mixed with a pledge to get back on track after the pyramid project has been completed, will yield a change of verdict on my part. In fact, as the manager/judge/warden of my boys, I actually want and expect them to appeal to my better judgment if I'm missing something. When they don't, but opt instead to throw a tantrum or political maneuvering, I assume they know my decision is correct and that they're trying to pull a fast one on me.

This same phenomenon occurs in the places where we work outside our homes.

A manager makes an unpopular policy decision that does not seem to be in the best interest of the company. Employees grumble to one another, peppering their manager's assistant with complaints that she passes along to the boss in the form of anecdotal information. Those same employees then try to find a way to thwart the policy by exploiting a technicality or lobbying others in the company to join their chorus of complaints. Eventually, chaos and dissent rise to a level where the leader must make a decision-relent to the pressure and look weak, or stand firm and cement his or her reputation as an authoritarian who is not concerned about employees. It's a no-win situation for the manager, which will produce a poor outcome for the company.

A better approach would be for employees to respectfully go to the manager directly and explain that they have the same general goals as the manager but that the new policy won't ultimately help them to accomplish those goals. As simple as that sounds, and possibly even naive, it is amazing to me how readily most leaders respond to the exertion of moral authority. But with one caveat.

Moral authority can't become moralistic authority. Too often we confuse the idea of taking a moral stand on an issue with taking a moralistic one. When we do that, when we come across as judgmental or condescending or angry, we run the risk of putting the person we're trying to influence on the defensive, which only encourages them to hold their ground and shut us out. The key to effective moral authority is taking a stand based on what is good while being kind and respectful and even empathic to the person we're trying to influence.

Now, moral authority certainly has its limits, especially in an organization or a society without common values. And it cannot force an excessively stubborn, insecure or ignorant leader to do

something they don't want to do. However, most of us fail to even consider using moral authority without knowing with confidence that the stubbornness, ignorance or insecurity of a leader is really insurmountable.

I realize that all of this sounds extremely simple and obvious. Which begs the question, 'why don't we do this more?' Sometimes we're afraid that it won't work and that we'll be punished. This is usually an exaggerated fear. Sometimes we assume that the leader who made the decision must have considered every option and chose the one they did carefully, and with conviction. This is very often an inaccurate and unfair assumption. But more often than not, I think we simply fail to realize that exercising moral authority is even an option, one that is in everyone's best interest, especially the leader's.

— JUNE 2008

Neighborhoods, Homes and Office Space

My dad used to say that littering is the first stage of crime.

What he meant was that when people don't keep their neighborhoods clean, they lose a sense of pride and personal responsibility. As the appearance of their environment continues to erode, a subtle but undeniable spiral occurs. People lose hope, their behavior becomes more irresponsible, the neighborhood gets worse, and eventually a town—or even a society—begins to crumble.

Beyond the social and psychological implications of my dad's philosophy—one that always made sense to me—it also speaks to the powerful impact that a physical environment can have on human beings. As simple as it may seem, the structure and appearance of a home or a neighborhood or a workplace has a profound influence on how the people who live or work there behave.

Imagine if your home were designed with spacious, palatial bedrooms and a miniscule family room. Would you be surprised to find that the interaction of family members decreased and ultimately impacted the unity of your family? Of course not. Yet somehow, most organizations fail to understand the impact that their physical structure has on the dynamics of employees.

The biggest problem with traditional office space is what it suggests about the importance of individual versus collective work. By placing greater emphasis on privacy than openness and collaboration, companies unconsciously encourage people to see their work as being primarily individual. Whether we're talking about line employees in cubicles or senior executives in walled offices, workers are almost trained to seek out greater separation and space.

On first glance, this might seem understandable, even natural. Human beings crave their own territory, or according to Maslow, shelter. But is that something we want to honor at work? In some cases, the answer is 'yes'. A few professions certainly lend themselves to individual focus and privacy and separation. But outside of writers and inventors and monks, not many come to mind.

Most jobs, and especially those that revolve around leadership, are social by nature and should be done in groups. Which means that the higher you go up the food chain within an organization, the more true this should be. And yet, the higher a manager rises in most organizations the more likely he or she is to be allocated an office, suggesting that his or her job is primarily about doing isolated thinking or planning. Or perhaps communicating via e-mail.

So, am I suggesting a radical departure from tradition, one in which executives sit in big, open areas with their teams, going into private rooms only on occasions when it is necessary? Well, I guess I am. Frankly, I don't see a better option. Until leaders are forced to interact with one another as a rule rather than an exception, they will continue to under-communicate and under-collaborate, creating cascading problems throughout the rest of the organizations they manage.

What I'm not suggesting, however, is the creation of funky offices with coffee bars or ping pong tables or spiral slides that connect one floor to another. Those are gimmicks which don't address the real problem created by too much privacy and separation. Neither am I suggesting that restructuring our offices become some sort of protest against hierarchy. The reason to move away from closed offices to more open designs is not about aesthetics or rebellion against authority. It is simply about creating an environment of where communication and teamwork have the best chance to thrive.

Now, if an organization is not truly committed to making teamwork a reality, then my suggestions here probably won't amount to much. Simply putting people in close proximity cannot substitute for a cultural shift toward trust and healthy conflict and transparency. But perhaps moving people out of their offices and into the light will be just what the organization needs to ignite their appreciation for the power of teamwork. And even if it doesn't, it will probably reduce real estate costs.

— MAY 2008

The Danger of Shiny New Things

I'm sure it's natural for people to be fascinated with acquiring new things. Whether we're talking about physical possessions like homes or cars or toys, or more conceptual assets like knowledge or technology or business strategies, we seem to highly value what we don't have, especially when it is novel.

I suppose this is understandable—even good—in a society that values progress and innovation. However, there is a cost to overemphasizing and over-valuing all things new, a cost that goes beyond obvious concerns about greed and over-consumption. When we are in constant pursuit of acquiring more of the latest and greatest, we usually diminish or dilute the power of what we already have.

My twin boys turn ten years old this month, and as I ponder what gift to give them, I realize that what they probably need more than anything is more time to play with the things they already have, things they haven't begun to fully use or enjoy. Giving them something new may not make them much happier, and may actually cause them distress. You've seen this dilemma on Christmas morning as your children sit in the midst of their own FAO Schwartz store, slipping into a toy-overload coma, overwhelmed by the choices they have and seemingly unable to process it all. If you're like me, you probably chastised yourself and vowed to your spouse that "next year we should give them just ONE present."

This same phenomenon affects us as leaders of organizations too. But rather than toys, the objects of our desire usually involve knowledge or information. Most leaders I work with grow bored easily, and are in constant pursuit of strategies, ideas, trends—even employees—that will somehow transform their organizations. Unfortunately, they haven't come close to fully tapping the strategies, ideas, trends or employees that they already have, and yet they discard those untapped assets in exchange for new ones.

On a personal level, I've experienced this phenomenon too. I've recently come to the conclusion that I should stop reading so many new books and magazine articles. Instead, I should go retrieve the top ten books and articles that I've already read, and start re-reading them again and again. After all, I've forgotten most of what I've learned in those books, and I'm certainly not using or tapping into more than a fraction of what they have to offer. Instead, I'm pursuing more and more new material, which only crowds out the space in my brain to recall and put to use the tried and true goodness of what I've already learned.

Why do we do this? Perhaps we want to stay current. Or we don't want to feel out of touch. But I think it is based more in pride of knowing things than in real pursuit of excellence, integrity and discipline.

Don't think that the irony of all this is lost on me, an author who writes a new book every few years and who wants people to buy and read them. But I cannot deny that one of my favorite quotes comes from the author Samuel Johnson who said that "people need to be reminded more than they need to be instructed." I suppose what he really meant was that we already have plenty of information. We just need to use it.

At the risk of going a little long, let me provide another example of the power of resisting all things new. This one is grounded in the world of corporate strategy.

There is a regional chain of quick-service (a.k.a. fast food) restaurants on the west coast called In-N-Out Burger. If you've never lived or spent much time in California, Nevada or Arizona, you might not know about In-N-Out, but it's a sixty year old company that has a cult-like following among people who like fresh, delicious hamburgers.

What's amazing about In-N-Out is that during their history they've almost never changed their menu. All they serve are cheeseburgers, hamburgers, french fries (one size only), milkshakes (chocolate, vanilla and strawberry, one size only), and soft drinks.

Imagine the temptations that the executives at In-N-Out have felt over the years to add something new. In addition to wanting to take advantage of trends and fads, they very easily could have decided they were bored offering the same menu. Why not add a chicken sandwich? Or a shamrock shake in March? Or a Mexican-pizza-melt? Every other restaurant is adding new items to keep customers interested. Weren't they worried they'd fall behind?

They've always said 'no', and kept their focus on making the freshest, most consistent high quality hamburger in the world—or at least in this part of the world. And they've never been willing to dilute their focus on that by chasing something shiny and new. They believe that there are plenty of people out there who want great hamburgers, and they're okay with those people driving to another restaurant when they are craving something else. That requires great restraint and a real appreciation for what they already have.

I should end this now so that it doesn't go too long. Besides, I have to go buy my boys a birthday present. Maybe I'll get them sweaters.

— APRIL 2008

The Greatest Leader

I have been asked on a number of occasions, by journalists and curious clients, whom I believe to be the greatest leader in America. And I usually respond with my own question. "Are you asking for the name of a famous leader?" This usually leads to a fair amount of confusion, until I explain that the best leader in the world is probably relatively obscure.

You see, I believe that the best leader out there is probably running a small or medium-sized company in a small or medium-sized town. Or maybe they're running an elementary school or a church. Moreover, that leader's obscurity is not a function of mediocrity, but rather a disdain for unnecessary attention and adulation. He or she would certainly prefer to have a stable home life, motivated employees, and happy customers—in that order—over public recognition.

A skeptic might well respond, "But if this person really were the greatest leader, wouldn't his or her company eventually grow in size and stature, and become known for being great?" And the answer to that fine question would be, "Not necessarily."

A great company should achieve its potential and grow to the size and scale that suits its founders' and owners' and employees' desires, not to mention the potential of its market. It may very well wildly exceed customer expectations and earn a healthy profit by doing so, but not necessarily grow for the sake of growing.

Unfortunately, we live in a world where bigger is often equated with better and where fame and infamy are all too often considered to be one and the same. And so we mistakenly come to believe that if we haven't seen a person's picture on the cover of *Businessweek* or in a dot-matrixed image in the *Wall Street Journal*, then they can't possibly be the best.

Consider for a moment those high profile leaders we do read about in the newspaper and see on television. Most, but not all, of them share an overwhelming desire and need for attention. You'll find them in all kinds of industries, but most prevalently in politics, media, and big business. Look hard enough at them, and there is a decent chance you'll discover people who have long aspired to be known as great leaders. These are the same people who also value public recognition over real impact. And based on my experience, you might also find that they'll be more highly regarded by strangers and mere acquaintances than by the people who work and live with them most closely.

The truth is, our greatest leaders usually don't aspire to positions of great fame or public awareness. They choose instead to lead in places where they can make a tangible, meaningful difference in the lives of the people they are called to serve. The challenges and consequences of their decisions are no less difficult or important than those of higher profile leaders, even if they don't quite qualify for a cover story in *TIME* Magazine.

— MARCH 2008

Teamwork, Leadership and Suffering

One of the most prevailing approaches to modern life, if not the predominant one, is the desire to avoid suffering. So much of our lives—and our economy—is involved in finding ways to get through our days without having to face the physical and emotional difficulties that are ultimately inevitable.

Evidence of this can be found in everything from the existence of hundreds of types of pain relievers (Extra Strength Tylenol Cold Gel Caps for Left-handed Children) to the bogus advertisements for miraculous weight loss solutions (Eat All You Want and Never Exercise!) to the preponderance of self-help books encouraging us to avoid guilt and personal responsibility for our actions by assigning blame and responsibility to a parent, teacher or family pet.

Of course this is understandable. None of us seeks out opportunities to suffer, and so none of us is immune from the temptation to avoid it. However, our inability to understand the inevitability and necessity of suffering has its costs.

When people fear suffering more than they should, they ironically experience unnecessary anguish and stress. Beyond that, some would say that worrying actually increases the likelihood that what is being feared will happen. Finally, our distaste for suffering makes it difficult for us to benefit from its effects, and from realizing the benefits that it yields when we emerge on the other side.

This is certainly true when it comes to teamwork and leadership, although a better term for suffering might be discomfort. All too often, team leaders and members operate under the assumption that success is dependent on never having to deal with a moment of interpersonal awkwardness or pain. This, of course, makes it virtually impossible—no, it makes it completely impossible—to achieve any real breakthroughs in building a team.

Every great team must suffer a little, and sometimes a lot, in order to achieve greatness. It must confront, experience and struggle with uncomfortable and relationship-threatening moments of conflict and confusion, and then it must work through those moments by demonstrating interpersonal courage, persistence and forgiveness. By doing so, it establishes levels of trust that simply cannot be otherwise achieved.

For those of us who are tempted to be skeptical about this, to continue searching for a team-building process that is painless and discomfort-free, we should look at family and marriage to give us clarity. When we realize that no great family or marriage can be formed—or maintained—without the willingness to enter the danger of interpersonal conflict and discomfort, we may begin to appreciate the importance of doing so on our teams.

Ironically, by doing so, a team will begin to diminish the level of awkwardness that it experiences, as well as the length of time that a given situation lasts. Most important of all, it will create an environment of honest, natural communication and interaction. And that is worth a lot more than the false benefits of avoiding discomfort in the first place.

— FEBRUARY 2008

The Law of Thirds

There is a model that I really love to share with clients because it always provokes an exceptionally strong reaction from them, a terrific mixture of revelation and relief. I wish I knew who to attribute the model to, because it is as powerful as it is simple.

What I'm talking about is something called the "law of thirds," and here's how it works.

Imagine that you are leading an organization of some kind. You might be a CEO of a company, or a manager with a department full of employees. Or you might be a pastor serving a congregation, or a principal with a host of children and parents in your school. This could even apply if you are a coach or a teacher or an elected representative in a local civic organization.

Whatever the case, you can divide your constituents into three segments: "supporters" (not 'yes people', but generally reasonable folks who want what is best for the organization), "naysayers" (generally unreasonable folks who always seem to complain), and "undecideds" (people in the middle who aren't quite sure which side to join). Incidentally, I don't think the three segments break into equally sized parts. I've usually found that there is a fairly sizable group of supporters, an even larger number of undecideds, and a relatively small collection of naysayers.

Unfortunately, the naysayer group manages to portray itself as being much larger than it actually is, like an animal flaring its mane to mislead and scare off a predator. The way that small groups do this within organizations is by continually demanding more time from leaders, and by protesting more loudly than the other two groups.

Now, the real power of the law of thirds lies in the choice it presents for leaders, and the starkly different ramifications of those choices.

Choice #1: Pleasing the Naysayers—By focusing attention on trying to win over the naysayers—something many of us 'pleasers' do—we end up giving them more oxygen than they deserve. Not only does this encourage them, it also provokes the undecideds to join the chorus of complainers when they realize that it's the best way to get the attention of the leader. And if that isn't scary enough, catering to the naysayers eventually pushes the very best supporters out the door in search of an organization where their loyalty and cooperation will be rewarded.

Choice #2: Assuming the Best—When we make the better decision and choose to focus our energy and attention on supporters, we drain the oxygen from the naysayers and provoke the undecideds to join the ranks of the supporters. And we end up encouraging the very worst of the naysayers to leave on their own, saving the organization valuable time and money. And if that sounds harsh, consider that we are helping them choose to find a place where they won't be so perpetually unhappy, if that is at all possible.

But what exactly does it mean to focus on the supporters? It doesn't mean we ignore the naysayers, per se. It is more about communicating to the entire organization as if everyone were reasonable and positive and generally interested in the greater good. That means we have to learn to smile at the naysayers, thank them for their input, and explain without apology or condescension that the organization is heading in a certain direction based on what's in the best interests of the whole.

And here's the amazing part; even some of the naysayers will eventually become supporters when they realize that chronic complaining doesn't work. Ironically, this can only happen when we stop trying to win them over. I guess that's yet another example of the power of tough love, something that pleasers like me sometimes struggle to do.

⌐ JANUARY 2008

The Best Gift a Manager Can Give an Employee

As we approach Christmas, it is natural for us to think of giving, though all too often in material terms.

Well, if you're a manager, and you'd like to give your employees something that will outlast any cookie basket or gift certificate or desk accessory you can order on-line, then I have just the thing for you.

It is remarkably simple and requires no money. It costs only a little time, and perhaps a bit more courage and vulnerability than managers are sometimes prepared to spend. But trust me, it's worth it.

These concepts are outlined in my new book, *The Three Signs of a Miserable Job*. To overcome the Three Signs here's what you need to do:

First, get to know your people better than you know them today. Take an interest in what is going on in their lives and find out what their dreams and passions are, both professionally and personally. The only caveat is that you have to be genuinely interested. If you haven't done this much before and you're afraid that it will feel weird to start now, do it anyway. Your employees want it, need it and will thank you for it.

Second, talk to them about how their job impacts the lives of others—customers, vendors, colleagues, even you!—in some way, large or small. Help them understand that their work matters, to someone, and that without them, others would suffer.

Finally, help them figure out how to best measure and gauge how effectively they are doing their jobs, especially in terms of the impact they have on others. Give them the ability to determine for themselves whether they are succeeding or not, and free them from depending on your subjective opinion for a sense of accomplishment or esteem.

Now, any one of these things alone would make a nice management gift, but together they become the most important quality any person yearns for in their jobs: fulfillment. Without them, employees cannot help but become miserable.

If all of this sounds a bit easy, or even touchy-feely, let me reassure you that neither is true. First, it will require a great deal of courage and selflessness on the part of a manager who will at times feel disingenuous, embarrassed or incompetent. And the only way to work through this is to do it anyway, knowing that those feelings are bound to arise and that you are going to endure them for the sake of your employees.

As for this being touchy-feely, ask yourself if productivity, morale and retention are touchy-feely. And more importantly, ask yourself whether tolerating a little touchy-feeliness—if that were the case—would be a reasonable price to pay for giving your employees a sense of appreciation, fulfillment and meaning at work.

By beginning the process—and it is certainly a process—of removing anonymity, irrelevance and immeasurement from the work lives of your employees, you will be giving your people a gift that will last far beyond this wonderful season, and that will impact their families and friends in profound, life-changing ways.

— WINTER 2007

 The content from this article was based on Pat's book, *The Three Signs of a Miserable Job*. For more information on the book, model and free tools, please visit www.tablegroup.com.

The Journey

I am glad to report that *The Three Signs of a Miserable Job* made the *New York Times* and *Wall Street Journal* best-seller lists during these past weeks and month, and I want to thank our friends and family and "cousins" of The Table Group who went out and purchased copies of the book right after it hit the shelves. Your support means a great deal to me and everyone at The Table Group, and we wish we could thank you all individually.

In addition to making those lists right out of the gate—something that has never happened with any of our other books—sales seem to be growing. I have never received so much e-mail from readers and I'm glad to report that so far, it's all been very positive.

Of course the most important part of this is the potential it has to make a difference. Given the amount of time that people spend at work, the ability of managers to positively impact the lives of their employees by avoiding the three signs is truly extraordinary. Our hope is the book continues to do well so that, manager by manager, organizations can transform their cultures and the lives of their employees.

THE JOURNEY

All of this reminds me of a lesson we've been learning since the founding of The Table Group, which happened almost 10 years ago to this day. Back then, we could not have imagined what would happen to us over the next decade. Every little step along the way seemed to exceed our expectations and leave us saying to ourselves, "even if it never gets better than this, it's been awesome."

I remember how excited we were when we first realized that we could sustain a small consulting business and pay our bills. And how ecstatic we were when a publisher agreed to publish *The Five Temptations of a CEO*. And then, when it sold 5,000 copies, well, what more could we want?

I guess the point I'm trying to make is that we tried to avoid getting ahead of ourselves, yearning for some kind of extraordinary end game to play out. We usually enjoyed, appreciated and were amazed by every incremental accomplishment, and in those times when we failed to do that, we usually struggled.

Sometimes I meet people who have great aspirations but who are so laser focused on their ultimate goal that they never really feel a sense of accomplishment or appreciation along the way. Ironically, their desire for greater success often impedes their ability to attain it.

But don't get me wrong. I'm not advocating complacency or the absence of setting big goals. We certainly spent time at The Table Group putting together a vision of what we might some day achieve. It's just that I think it's unwise to allow your sense of success to depend upon achieving some long term, ideal goal. By appreciating every moment as though it might be the final rung on your ladder of success, you can pursue other goals with a sense of joy and confidence, rather than stress and fear.

And so, as we look back at these past ten years, we're keenly aware that we've been blessed far more than we deserved. We are grateful that we have been able to make a living doing something we love with people we love, and we are grateful for all of your help, large and small, along the way.

— FALL 2007

Incentives

It occurred to me recently that the most meaningful, rewarding and impactful work I do is frequently free of charge. It's not that I don't enjoy the paid projects. In fact, I very much appreciate the fact that most of my clients pay me, and I am blessed to truly like the work I do for them.

Whether I'm consulting to a church organization or giving a talk to a non-profit, the pro bono projects are usually among my favorites. Beyond the dilemma this poses for the CFO of our little firm, I think this is a phenomenon worth pondering.

The first explanation that comes to mind is a relatively obvious one: I already have a passion for these organizations, and so it stands to reason that I would derive a greater sense of satisfaction from my work. But I think there's more to it than that, and it has to do with something I learned in a social psychology class during college.

Researchers did an experiment in which they asked people on the street to provide some sort of assistance to a stranger. As it turned out, a high percentage of those who were asked agreed to help. Then the experimenters changed the stakes and added a nominal financial incentive to the subjects request, and found that a much smaller percentage of people agreed to help.

The point of the experiment was that people are more enthusiastic about doing something when they believe it is right or good, than when they calculate their economic self-interest. What is more, offering more money to someone who is already committed can actually decrease their incentive to work harder, as it makes them feel bought rather than appreciated. I'm thinking that there's a lesson here for most organizations, non-profits and for profits alike.

MONEY VS. PASSION

Before I go any further, let me make it clear that compensation is a very real and important part of most jobs. Everyone needs money to live, and everyone wants to be compensated fairly.

However, some people don't really work for money. Once they get enough—and yes, that varies from person to person—they lose much of their financial motivation for working harder. The truth is, money has definite limits as a motivator, and thus, is referred to as a "satisfier."

Passion for a cause, on the other hand, has few limits. People who believe in what they're doing are going to continue to give more and more even when there is no additional financial benefit. That is true whether the person is doing altruistic work at a church or a non-profit, crunching numbers at a bank, doing research for a pharmaceutical company or playing basketball for an NBA team.

And yet, we continue to focus so much of our management attention on money, for two likely reasons. First, no one ever turns down a raise, so we mistakenly assume that money is the primary motivator. Second, money is easier to measure than passion or meaning.

Ironically, by offering more money to someone who is really lacking a sense of connection to their work, not only are we getting diminishing marginal returns for our compensation dollars, we may actually be getting negative ones.

THE JOHN STOCKTON EFFECT

Consider an example from the world of sports. It is common for a player in the last year of his contract to give extra effort on the field or the court, knowing that a statistical improvement will enhance his negotiation position and net him and his agent a bigger contract. Unfortunately for many teams who agree to those contracts, that player often chooses to coast as soon as the ink is dry, at least until he's in the final year of that contract. The list of players who fit this description is long.

Then consider John Stockton, the all-time assist leader in the NBA. That's right. He had more assists than Magic Johnson or Bob Cousy or Jason Kidd, and is considered one of the fifty best players in the history of the game.

John Stockton did not have an agent, but instead chose to negotiate his own contracts. He didn't get paid quite as much as other players of similar or lesser talent, because he was already making more money than he could ever need. But because he felt so connected to his team, the Utah Jazz,

and such an important part of Salt Lake City, Stockton played harder than virtually any other player in the league, and stayed his entire career in Utah.

Is Stockton an anomaly? Maybe, but not as much as cynics would think. I honestly believe there are plenty of other players in the league (Tim Duncan comes to mind) and employees in your organization, who are like him. They might not come right out and say it, but what they're looking for more than money is a sense of belonging and purpose and passion.

And so we have a choice. We can either focus our efforts on finding a way to give employees passion and purpose, and watch their productivity soar. Or we can pay them more money and hope that their performance doesn't tank as a result.

Here's another way to think about this, one that I heard at a recent conference during a conversation with the Chief Operating Officer of Taco Bell. He may have summarized my point here best of all when he said, "We need to treat all of our employees, regardless of what kind of organization we work in, as volunteers." Sometimes the most ridiculous sounding things make the most sense.

— SPRING 2007

Management and Youth Soccer

Last spring was the big draft. You may have heard about it.

No, I'm not referring to the NFL draft that took place in April, or the NBA edition in June. I'm talking about the Mustang Boys' Under-nine Soccer draft in Danville, California. That's right. As ridiculous as it sounds, I'm talking about eight-year-old boys, third graders, actually getting drafted to play "competitive soccer". And the process by which they're evaluated, rated and selected is a sight to see.

Imagine a soccer field surrounded by clip-board toting coaches (myself included) who are taking detailed notes as they watch little boys run and kick and dribble and scrimmage against one another. Afterward, those coaches sit down around a table and take turns selecting twelve players for their respective teams.

Luckily for me, I don't know a great deal about soccer. I played very little of the sport as a grade-schooler, though I've coached my sons' six and seven-year-old teams. But to be fair, the nature of the game played by my boys' pee wee teams more closely resembled a revolt within a prison than it did a sporting event.

I say that I'm lucky to be ignorant of soccer because it forced me to confront a brutal fact: I was going to be at a distinct competitive disadvantage when it came to assessing the technical skills of the munchkins on my list of draftable players. You see, the other coaches in the league have all played soccer at collegiate, professional or semi-professional levels, and they appreciate the nuances of the sport the way I do basketball or baseball. They are the type of people who not only understand the off-sides rule, but actually like it!

Anyway, to mitigate my soccer naivete, I made a decision that was motivated mostly out of desperation, with a little inspiration mixed in. In essence, I decided to completely change the criteria I would use to evaluate and select players for my team (which, by the way, is called The Swarm).

So, I took the official evaluation form that was given to me before the try-outs, and crossed out the provided category descriptions like "speed", "field awareness", "touch" and "power", and replaced them with others like "attitude", "hustle" and "skill" and "parents". Of course, that meant I would have to focus on observing different things than my peers would be looking for during the tryouts.

For instance, instead of spending most of my time looking at the players' feet, I tended to watch how they treated one another. I wanted to see how they responded when the instructor asked them to help move one of the portable goals or a bag of soccer balls to the other side of the field. I also watched the way they interacted with their parents during breaks. Were they respectful or inattentive? And I wanted to see how hard they played on the field. Did they only run when the ball came to them, or did they get involved and help out on defense?

During breaks I might slyly approach one of the kids and ask, "Hey there Billy, how do you like school?" or "What's your favorite subject?" And I was looking for someone who would say, "Yeah, I like school a lot", or "I like math, but not spelling so much." What I didn't want was a blank stare or an answer like "nah, the only thing I like is recess."

Anyway, when the tryouts were over, my assistant coach (who never played or coached soccer before) and I ranked the players from top to bottom, according to our largely attitudinal criteria. When the draft began, we nervously waited our turn. By the time the draft had ended, we had picked more of our top "prospects" than we could have imagined, and assembled a team that we felt had a very high likelihood of being positive and coachable.

Now, don't misunderstand this philosophy of mine for altruism or nobility. I have a competitive streak too, and I wanted our team to be successful. Certainly, I value character-building and fitness more than winning, but I didn't want to field a team full of nice kids who couldn't score goals. And I would be lying if I said we didn't pay any attention to the basic athletic ability of the players we selected. But those skills took a distant back seat to attitude and demeanor.

As the season approached, my assistant coach and I wondered how much talent we had on the team. We hoped we'd have at least one good goalie and a few natural scorers. By the time our first

practiced was upon us, we didn't know what to expect. So we crossed our fingers, skimmed through "Soccer For Dummies", and began the season.

That was six weeks ago. As of the writing of this article, we've played a little less than half of our games, and a few things have become crystal clear to us.

First, our team is a team. They treat each other well, encourage one another, and seek out collective attention more than individual praise. Second, they're having fun. They don't complain about practices, and they enjoy being together. Third, their parents are having fun. Many of them have approached me and my assistant coach to tell us how pleasantly surprised they are about the positive environment on the team, and how much they enjoy being on the sideline with the other parents.

What about the soccer? So far, so good. We've only lost three of thirteen games, and we've outscored our opponents 24-7. Of course, that is not near as important as the other factors (I have to keep reminding myself and the other parents about that), but it's a nice confirmation that our attitudinal approach is as viable on the field as it is off of it. It will be interesting to see how the team handles itself when we inevitably lose a few games in a row.

I'd like to say that this early success of the team is a result of great coaching and tactical training. But that just isn't the case. The fact is, as Jim Collins points out in *Good to Great*, getting the right people on the bus is the first critical step toward building a great organization of any kind.

Once the bus is full, then it's all about getting the right people in the right seats (or in our case, the right players in the right positions). But selecting the people who fit your culture, whether they are eight-year-old soccer players, senior executives, teachers or church volunteers, is the first critical step.

Why? Because it's a lot easier to teach a humble, hard-working young man how to play goalie than it is to teach a spectacular athlete how to listen and put the team before himself. I'm guessing that applies to the organization where you work. Not the goalie part. Well, you know what I mean.

— FALL 2006

If Everything is Important...

In my latest book, *Silos, Politics, and Turf Wars*, I present a model for achieving alignment across departments within an organization, and eliminating unnecessary and costly infighting. A pleasant by-product of that model is improved prioritization for companies, something that is sorely lacking for so many of them.

Most of the companies I have encountered over the years seem addicted to having a long list of "top" priorities. As a result, they're unable to focus on any one of them out of fear that doing so will somewhat increase the likelihood that others will fall by the wayside.

And so, the vast majority of these organizations end up peanut-buttering their energy and attention across so many different activities that none of them seem to be any more imperative than another. Hence the phrase, "if everything is important, then nothing is."

Managers and employees alike are left scratching their heads as they try to decipher where to focus their limited time and resources, ultimately defaulting to whatever activity is most urgent or most tactically relevant to their isolated jobs.

I've found that the best way to demonstrate the problem—and illustrate a solution—is to start close to home. In fact, at home itself.

ESTABLISH A THEMATIC GOAL

Every family can relate to the craziness of trying to manage a long list of competing priorities. Keeping the kids active versus spending more time at home as a family. Saving money for college vs. taking nice vacations. Maintaining date night with your spouse vs. carving out one-on-one time with the kids. Working harder to earn more money for the family vs. coaching the little league team. The list is endless, leaving us breathless and frustrated, and all-too-often, feeling defeated.

And that's where a thematic goal can be so helpful for a family. For those who haven't read *Silos, Politics, and Turf Wars*, a thematic goal is a rallying cry that gives people in an organization an

unambiguous sense of what is most important during a given period of time, usually 6-12 months. Let's take a look at how this might apply in our homes.

Imagine that you have three boys, and that you are living somewhere close to the edge of chaos. Between baseball and school and church and soccer and cub scouts and gymnastics and homework and housework and office work and yard work—there is little time for sleep, let alone family management. Now imagine that you or your wife becomes pregnant. I cannot only imagine this, but I have recently experienced it.

I thought it would be a good opportunity to put my theory of a thematic goal to the test. Immediately, my wife, Laura, and I agreed what our thematic goal would be: Prepare For Baby #4. Easy enough. The sub-text of this goal was to keep our family sane and ensure that it had a fighting chance to stay that way going forward.

Keep in mind that there were other things we wanted to do during that time period. Like redo the front yard or take up pilates. But it was also clear to us that preparing for the arrival of another child was far and away the most important priority, and that nothing should prevent us from doing so. If that meant that the front yard would be a jungle for another six months and our inability to touch our toes without bending our knees would continue for awhile, then so be it.

The next question we had to answer about our priority was, how? How do we go about doing this? Do we walk around every day mumbling the mantra "Prepare For Baby #4", "Prepare For Baby #4"? Or do we plaster "PFB #4" signs all over the house to remind us? Only if we want our friends to make fun of us.

MAKE IT REAL

The first thing we needed to do was decide what we would need to accomplish in order to say that we had, indeed, adequately prepared for our new arrival. After some thought and conversation, we decided that there were four general categories (I call them defining objectives in the book, because they define what is required to accomplish the thematic goal).

- Finish a house remodel that was behind schedule and had the potential for dragging on far into the future. We couldn't have construction taking place under the same roof where a newborn was living.

- Outsource a few household responsibilities that we would not be able to continue doing, and that weren't core to being good parents. In our case, that meant a little more help with house cleaning and some external financial management support.

- Make our eight year old twins self-sufficient in terms of making breakfast, dressing themselves for school, taking showers, etc, because we could no longer afford to supervise these activities. And our three and a half year old would need to make a major step up in terms of discipline, involving sleep hours, tantrums and television.

- Purge our house of the countless "things" that we didn't really need to have, in order to make room for an influx of baby supplies.

So that was our basic structure for our rallying cry. If we could manage to make progress in each of these areas, we would be well on our way to sanely welcoming our new little boy. By the way, Michael was born on April 7, healthy and happy, thank God.

This concept of having a thematic goal and defining objectives is a simple one, and therein lies its power. It provides us with a manageable list of relevant issues that we can get our hands and minds around over an extended period of time. And just as importantly, it gives us permission to ignore other issues that would otherwise compete for our attention.

For most of us, whether we're running a household, a junior high school, a church or a corporation, our biggest challenge quickly becomes deciding what NOT to do. And when our heads hit the pillow at night, we don't want to be thinking about a long list of unrelated issues and e-mails and complaints that just happen to have found their way onto our desks.

If we're going to be losing sleep, we at least ought to be focused on those issues that truly matter most. And if there is no such list, then we're going to be losing a lot of sleep with little or nothing to show for it.

— SPRING 2006

 The content from this article was based on Pat's book, *Silos, Politics and Turf Wars*. For more information about the book, model and free tools, please visit www.tablegroup.com.

The Upside of Crisis

No one hopes for a crisis, and rightly so. Certainly this applies to teams and organizations. Most leaders would probably say one of their primary responsibilities is to prevent a crisis from occurring.

However, I have found that a powerful lesson for organizations can be found smack dab in the middle of a crisis. It isn't uncommon for a leader to say, "our team has never pulled together more than when we were facing a crisis." Maybe it's the prospect of going out of business or dealing with a public relations catastrophe or even a natural disaster that causes people to rally.

And while this may not seem surprising, it begs the question, "why?" Why do people set aside their usual squabbles and petty politics in the midst of a crisis?

I found an answer while pondering which teams and organizations live in a perpetual state of crisis every day. Consider firefighters, emergency medical technicians (EMTs), and soldiers in the heat of a rescue mission or battle. These are certainly some of the least political and divisive teams that you'll ever find. For them, disagreement about budgets and lines of responsibility are inconceivable. Or even worse, deadly. And that's the point. When the stakes are clear and high—life or death— well-intentioned human beings can't help but focus on the overriding task at hand. Which is precisely what happens to companies in crisis: they focus around a compelling, over-arching goal.

In my newly released book, *Silos, Politics, and Turf Wars*, I ask the question, why wait for a crisis to rally your team or organization? Create a sense of sharing and a compelling purpose all the time. We call this rallying cry a thematic goal. This involves deciding the one thing that matters most in the organization and rallying your people around it. Who knows? You may find that by doing so, you'll avoid a crisis.

— WINTER 2006

 The content from this article was based on Pat's book, *Silos, Politics and Turf Wars*. For more information on the book, the model and free tools, please visit www.tablegroup.com.

Team Season

October is a good time to talk about teamwork, especially as it pertains to sports. Professional football and hockey are now in full swing, baseball is in the midst of the playoffs, and basketball, believe it or not, is already playing pre-season games.

And even if pro sports aren't your thing, you probably have a son or daughter or niece or nephew playing youth soccer, volleyball or football right now. As for me, I'm coaching a pack of seven year old boys on a soccer team.

All of this raises a question that may seem simple at first glance: why is sports such a common, and effective, metaphor for teamwork? Many people would say that it's because so many of us played youth sports. Then why not cub scout packs, or ballet companies, or marching bands? After all, those are basically teams, too. What makes sports so special?

Well, I think the answer has everything to do with the scoreboard. I believe the scoreboard is what makes an athletic contest compelling, and provides the context for teamwork.

A scoreboard provides players, coaches, officials and fans alike with the framework for why they should care about what is happening on the court or field. And it informs them about what needs to be done, in what period of time, and to what extent, in order for the team to succeed. Without a scoreboard, there is just too much room for ambiguity and interpretation about whether a team has succeeded, and what they need to do to get better next time.

Which is precisely why teams within organizations-starting at the top-need to do a better job of creating, and using, scoreboards to drive their actions. As obvious as all of this may seem, effective scoreboards aren't really being used correctly by executive teams in many of the organizations I've encountered. Most of them are either putting too little information, or too much, on their scoreboard, leaving people confused about how to affect the outcome of the game, or overwhelmed about how to interpret what is going on around them.

TOO LITTLE INFORMATION

So many organizations rely on revenue or profitability or stock price as the primary gauges for the success of their team. While these are certainly the ultimate measure of a company's performance, they are not particularly helpful in terms of day-to-day, or week-to-week decision making.

Relying on these metrics would be like a baseball team looking up at the scoreboard and seeing only one statistic-season standings. While tracking wins and losses is certainly critical for any team, it does not provide enough timely information about how any individual player can positively impact the near term performance of the organization. What is needed is more information, the kind that focuses, rallies and motivates people to adjust their behavior in a way that will give the team a better chance of winning.

Metrics like profitability, revenue and stock price don't adequately inform, drive or motivate performance because they involve too many contributing factors, and require too much time to determine meaningful trends. This leads people to either over-react to what they're seeing, or to get paralyzed as they see no connection between their short-term behavior and the long-term consequences of it.

TOO MUCH INFORMATION

Many well-intentioned executive teams go in the opposite direction in their quest for scoreboard clarity. They track as many metrics as they can get their hands on (detailed product quality specifications, region by region sales forecasts, advertising response rates, employee turnover), in the hope that they will leave no stone unturned. But this only overwhelms employees with statistics that are difficult to digest and interpret in a meaningful way. Ultimately, they start to tune out that data, leaving them with little context for their actions.

Consider a football team glancing at the scoreboard and trying to wade through everything from first downs and turnovers to penalty yards and player-by-player yardage statistics. As interesting as that data might be to a fan or sports writer, or even a coach with four hours to spare doing

post-game analysis, it would be next to useless for a coach or player on the field looking for information about what play to call next or whether they should call timeout.

JUST RIGHT

Sports scoreboards contain just enough information to help people on the field or court make informed decisions about how they can increase the odds of winning the game. This almost always includes a few simple metrics like the time remaining in the game, the number of timeouts the team has at its disposal, and of course, the score itself.

Like different industries, different sports have a few unique items on their scoreboards. Baseball, for instance, has strikes, balls and outs instead of time. Football has the down and yardage for a first down. Basketball tracks team fouls, and hockey displays penalty time. In each sport, however, there are only a handful of key categories. Dozens and dozens of other interesting statistics never find their way onto the scoreboard. They would only cloud the decision-making ability of coaches and players. Instead, they are left to analysts and planners for another time and place when that information might actually be helpful.

What is the right scoreboard for you? That will depend somewhat on the size of your organization as well as your industry. But whatever it is, it should be designed expressly to guide the actions of the company's leaders. That means the scoreboard will most likely contain between two and seven items that correspond to a period of time that is within your company's foreseeable and actionable horizon. Finally, the scoreboard should also be easily understandable by people deeper in the organization. That is, of course, if you want them to be focused around what really matters, and motivated to make a difference.

— FALL 2005

Three Profiles in Organizational Humility

There is nothing like humility in a leader to bring out the best in people. Humble leaders provoke levels of loyalty, commitment and performance that more ego-centric ones can't quite elicit or understand.

To a large extent, the same can be said of organizations. When combined with a clear sense of purpose and drive, humility can propel a seemingly ordinary company to achieve uncommon results, usually by creating an environment of teamwork and willingness to learn from mistakes.

Over the course of the past few years, I've been fortunate to have access to three very different world class organizations that impressed me with their humility and, frankly, surprised me. I was shocked because my observations seemed to contrast what their critics had led me to believe.

The first of these organizations is none other than Wal-Mart. Yes, Wal-Mart. I spent a day last year at their headquarters in Bentonville, Arkansas, and had no idea what I was in for.

Having heard again and again about how Wal-Mart was dominating and controlling the retail industry and mistreating employees, I was expecting to arrive at a main campus resembling one of the many high tech country clubs I've grown accustomed to seeing in the Silicon Valley. What I found in Bentonville was a collection of buildings that were neither uniform nor impressive, many of which seemed to be converted warehouses and strip-mall quality structures from the 1970s. I loved it! And there was no separate executive suite with a different set of standards.

These titans of industry were working in facilities that were no more comfortable or grand than those of the people who worked in their stores around the world. And inside those buildings, the stories were no different. Neat and clean, but more like a DMV than a palace. And the cafeteria where I had lunch reminded me of my junior high school.

But the humility at Wal-Mart went far beyond the physical environment. The people there were uniformly friendly, gracious and unpretentious. But don't misunderstand. They were also very bright and had levels of experience, education and knowledge rivaling any other corporation I had seen. But you would never know it by the way they treated one another. And everyone, from senior executives to the people running the cash registers in the cafeteria, were treated with the same levels of respect and kindness, all of which seemed to create an environment of genuine enthusiasm and commitment among employees.

As for their reaction to the barrage of criticism leveled at them by competitors and the media, they were neither bitter nor angry. Instead, they seemed genuinely open to finding any truth in the accusations so they could address them, and then determined to calmly set the record straight in the many areas where they were being unfairly accused.

The second organization that impressed me with its humility is the United States Military Academy at West Point. I had a chance to visit the campus for two days last year with my father, and we were each overwhelmed by what we experienced.

From the general who ran the school itself and the officers and professors who taught the courses to the cadets and enlisted men who worked security at the front gate, humility was the dominant and undeniable trait shared by all. And this went far beyond the *yessirs* and *nosirs* that one would expect to find at a military institution.

Here were some of the very best and brightest young people in the nation, with outstanding academic, extracurricular and athletic backgrounds, and you would have thought that none of them had seen their own resumes.

And like Wal-Mart, people of every rank and age and gender were treated with uniform levels of respect and kindness. My father, who had served as an enlisted man in the army more than thirty years ago, was treated by three star generals as though he were their military peer.

So many people, who have never known a West Point cadet or visited the campus, assume that arrogance and macho must rule the day there. Nothing could be further from the truth. While there is certainly no lack of courage and character among the men and women who attend and

run the institution, none of them seems to have a need to prove that to anyone other than to themselves. God bless them for what they're doing.

The final organization I want to cite for its humility is a high school football team. Actually, it's not a team so much as it is a school and a sports program. I live near De La Salle High School, an all-male Christian Brothers institution that has become known for having the best high school football team in the history of the sport, or for that matter, any sport. Over the course of fifteen years, the team won 151 consecutive games and traveled extensively to play the best teams they could find.

I had heard many stories about the De La Salle football factory over the years, and the allegations of recruiting great players from faraway places to stack the deck in their favor. All of which led to my astonishment at what I would find when I attended a few of their games and came to know something about their coach and program, in general.

First, walking into their "stadium" is both a let-down and a breath of fresh air. The facility itself is tiny. Tiny. After more than twenty years of unparalleled success, most schools would have been tempted to construct a monument to football. Not De La Salle. You can drive by the school and pass the field and mistake it for a junior high school.

On top of that, there is no mention anywhere of the exploits of the football team. No championship signs. No shrine to their coaches or players. Nothing. The only meaningful tribute I've ever seen there was a painting of a player who was tragically murdered last year. And that's the thing about De La Salle. It's not about football, or championships, or fame. It's about the way people treat people.

I had a chance to hear the team's head coach speak at an event last year, and I can honestly say that I've never been moved so much by a talk. Coach Ladouceur was not stylishly dressed and was, by no means, a particularly eloquent or fiery or demonstrative speaker. Keep in mind that this is a guy who has been profiled on ESPN and in *Sports Illustrated*, and has had many of the nation's finest coaches at every level seek his advice. I would have expected even a bad high school football coach to be a little brash. But Ladouceur oozed humility.

Every statement he made had meaning, and almost none of it was about him. He talked about the fact that he considers himself a religion teacher and character mentor first and foremost, and that he does not and never will actively recruit kids to come to his school. He said he admires his players for having skills and talents and potential that he could only dream of. And there was no doubt in my mind that he meant every word he said.

What did I learn from Wal-Mart, West Point and De La Salle? That humility is powerful, but cannot be attained out of desire for power. It is its own aim, and its own reward. I also learned that one of the costs of being humbly successful is that others will throw stones at you, and that humility requires that you throw none back.

Finally, I realized that humble organizations are open to learning from others. Wal-Mart and West Point had asked me to come teach them about teamwork. As ridiculous as it seemed to me, they insisted that there is always more to learn. Which is what humility is all about.

— SUMMER 2005

Leaders Suffer

This is a good time of year to talk about suffering as it pertains to leadership.

Perhaps one of the biggest misconceptions that people have of great leaders is that they are the recipients of only wonderful benefits—fame, fortune, perks, attention—as a result of holding their position of power or influence. Often we focus on the accolades that leaders receive at the end of their career, in many cases even after they have died. The truth is, being a leader, at least a great one, is a largely sacrificial endeavor, one with far greater costs than benefits.

Part of the reason this misconception exists is that leaders are not encouraged, or even allowed, to acknowledge their pain and suffering. After all, in many organizations leaders earn a lot more money than the people they lead, and any discussion of their pain would elicit little sympathy.

Which is fine, because sympathy is not what leaders need most. What they do need is an understanding that all great leaders suffer, and that important accomplishments cannot be achieved without suffering. This has been true throughout history. What kind of suffering am I referring to?

Loneliness, rejection, unpopularity, blame and criticism. And while it is true that no one gets through life without experiencing all of these realities from time to time, great leaders put themselves in a position to get far more than their fair share, and with greater intensity.

Great leaders are often *lonely* because they do not give in to the temptation to vent their problems with others in the organization, deciding instead to carry those issues themselves. They experience *unpopularity* and *rejection* by making the difficult decisions that can temporarily alienate the people they lead. They invite *blame* and *criticism* by accepting responsibility for every failure in the organization while giving away credit for most successes.

In short, great leaders make the mission of the organization more important than their personal needs, which takes a very real toll on any human being. It leads to restless nights of sleep, strain on their families and questions about self-worth. And again, that's above and beyond the regular doses of these maladies that non-leaders experience.

Now, when people assume positions of leadership without expecting all of this, they set themselves up for substantial disillusionment and disappointment. And once that disappointment kicks in, they often find themselves tempted to compensate themselves through excessive financial or ego-related rewards.

In fact, this failure to understand the inherently sacrificial nature of leadership may well lie at the heart of the scandals that have made their way onto the front pages of our newspapers. Disappointed with the relatively unsatisfying personal economics of their jobs, CEOs look for love in all the wrong places. Fame. Fortune. Perks. Attention.

Truly great leaders overcome these temptations. They know that the only real, lasting reward for being a leader is the accomplishment of goals that result in the betterment of others. Even when that involves suffering.

So, whether you're the CEO of a Fortune 500 company, the head of a department within that company, an entrepreneurial leader of a small business, the principal of an elementary school or the minister of a church, remember that suffering is part of your job. And the next time you're in the midst of it, know that you're probably doing something important.

— SPRING 2005

Adrenaline Addiction

Einstein once said that the definition of stupidity is doing the same thing over and over and expecting different results. Sometimes, however, it isn't stupidity that causes this behavior, but something far more insidious and painful: addiction.

Many of the leaders I've worked with struggle with a deceptive addiction that hurts their organizations, their families, and their job satisfaction. I'm not talking about the need for drugs or alcohol, but rather another chemical, of sorts: adrenaline.

THE PROFILE

Executives with adrenaline addiction are the ones always pecking away at their Blackberries during meetings, talking on their cell phones during every five minute break of those meetings, and checking e-mail late at night. They go from meeting to meeting to meeting with no time in between for reflection or thought.

Always overwhelmed, adrenaline junkies seem to have a constant need for urgency, even panic, to get them through the day. They cannot grasp the race-driver's motto: you have to slow down to go fast. Instead, they keep their foot on the pedal at full throttle, convinced that any deceleration is a lost opportunity.

Like an alcoholic after a night of binge drinking, an adrenaline addict will often sit home at night wondering how life became so chaotic, and vowing to take back control the next day. And then that day begins and their addiction kicks in, giving them a sense of comfort even as it hurts them.

There is something particularly insidious about adrenaline addiction that makes it hard for many leaders to kick the habit. Unlike other addicts whose behaviors are socially frowned-upon, adrenaline addicts are often praised for their frantic activity, even promoted for it during their careers. And so they often wear their problem like a badge of honor, failing to see it as an addiction at all in spite of the pain it causes.

When confronted about their problem, adrenaline addicts (I'm a recovering one myself) will tell you about their endless list of responsibilities and all the people who need their attention. And while they'll often complain about their situation, they'll quickly brush off any constructive advice from spouses, friends or co-workers who 'just don't understand.'

THE COST

Of course, the first casualties of adrenaline addiction are the addicts themselves. As they get busier and busier, with no relief in sight, the rush from their addiction subsides and their job satisfaction starts to plummet. Activities that they once enjoyed, that they aspired to do for years, suddenly become drudgery, causing the quality of their work to drop, too. When they come to the conclusion that they're working harder than ever, with less results and personal satisfaction, frustration only increases.

But the addict is not the only victim of this problem. The rest of the organization finds itself whipped in different directions, seemingly at random, based on whatever issue is causing the leader's adrenaline to spike. Strategic planning goes out the window, replaced by reactivity and self-inflicted crisis management.

No one within the organization is spared from the effects of the addiction. The people who work directly for an addict must respond to—even enable—the addiction, and inevitably pass the panic down throughout the organization. The effect of this chain reaction is impressive to behold as employees three levels below can be seen scurrying aimlessly, all because of the adrenaline induced reaction of a leader at the top. Needless to say, morale in an adrenaline addicted organization suffers as employees wonder why they're doing what they're doing, and waiting for the next random command to come down the pike.

Of course, the personal life of an adrenaline addict is not immune from the problem, either. Decreased job satisfaction, increased stress and more time at the office affects families in profound and painful ways.

RECOVERY

So what can addicts do to combat this problem? First, they need to understand what kind of addict they are so that they can get to the root of their problem—because not all adrenaline addicts are the same. Here are the four types:

1. **The Accomplisher**—this is the classic type of adrenaline addict, the one who has an almost innate need to stay busy and cross things off a list in order to feel productive. They like to be able to measure daily progress in terms of what they have completed, even at the expense of the bigger, longer term view. Accomplishers are most susceptible to developing an adrenaline addiction because they are prone to take on more and more work.

2. **The Personal Deflector**—this is the type that uses their addiction to keep from assessing themselves and reflecting on their situation. They often have problems in their personal lives—or no personal life at all—and the last thing they want to do is face up to that. So they convince themselves that they have no time for their personal lives, which, sadly, only exacerbates the problem and prolongs the pain of dealing with it.

3. **The Organizational Deflector**—this type is like the previous one, except that the issue being avoided is trouble within the organization. Often times a CEO or senior executive of a struggling company convinces themselves and others that they are too busy to stop and take an honest look at the company's situation. As the company spirals, the adrenaline addict only works harder, trying to be convinced that the problem can be solved by working more hours at breakneck speed. They will do anything to avoid confronting the real problems, which are often more fundamental and require real change.

4. **The Dramatist**—some adrenaline addicts get a degree of satisfaction from their addiction, because it gives them an opportunity to draw attention to themselves and their plight. They repeatedly complain about their overwhelming situation, seemingly in search of admiration or pity from anyone who will listen.

These types of adrenaline addiction, though different, have some elements in common. Certainly, many addicts will see more than one type in their own behavior.

THE TREATMENT

But how do they overcome their addiction?

Like any other addiction, the first step is to acknowledge the problem, and to declare a desire to eliminate it. Until that happens, there is little or no hope of improvement.

The second step is for them to let their peers and subordinates know that they are trying to kick the habit, because many of these people have become enablers over the years and have learned to play to the person's addiction. Those people must be given explicit permission to stop enabling the behavior.

Finally, an adrenaline addict needs to confront whatever issue underlies their problem. For the Accomplisher, it may be a false need to prove that they are worthy of their job. For the Personal Deflectors, it will involve having the courage to look at their lives holistically and honestly, maybe with the help of a counselor of some kind. The Organizational Deflector needs to embrace what Jim Collins calls "the brutal facts" about the business. And the Dramatist probably needs to address a deeper issue in their lives, one that involves their self-esteem. They need to disconnect their personal needs from those of the organization.

What are the benefits of kicking an adrenaline habit? Executives who are not adrenaline addicts make purposeful decisions about how they spend their time and where they give their attention. They may be wildly busy at times, but they choose to be that way for limited periods of time because the situation truly warrants it.

Recovering addicts enjoy and understand the need to take a breath from time to time, to step back from their daily grind to assess and reflect where they are professionally, as well as personally. And just as importantly, they prevent their peers, their subordinates and their families from having to deal with the secondary affects of their addiction.

— FALL 2004

Hiring Problems

I continue to be amazed by the lack of rigor I see among managers, especially senior executives, who are hiring leaders to help run their companies. In spite of all the great books and studies out there about the benefits of behavioral interviewing and the need to "hire for fit, train for skill," I am constantly confronted by evidence that suggests people are still hiring the old-fashioned way: for resume skills.

In so many cases this leads to hiring people who might be "rock stars" in their own right, but who end up creating political problems that disrupt the team, and ultimately, the health of the organization. I'm wondering if many executives aren't merely giving lip service to the cultural hiring school of thought, and privately writing it off as some touchy-feely campaign of behavioral psychologists.

If we need any evidence of the importance of assembling team members to work well together, we can look at the NBA Championship series that ended last month.

The Lakers were considered to be perhaps the best collection of talent the league had ever seen. That's tough to dispute when you consider they had four certain Hall of Fame players, and more importantly, two of the top ten players of all time (this is hard for me to admit because I'm not a Lakers fan). However, I'm not disappointed to tell you that those "rock star" players were resoundingly defeated by the Detroit Pistons, a collection of supposed role players, cast-offs and under-achievers who meshed together and played like a team.

Who is ultimately responsible for all of this? A man named Joe Dumars, who is the General Manager of the Detroit Pistons, and who was a quiet team player in his own career. He selected a coach and players who complemented one another and who fit a cultural model (toughness, hard-work, unselfishness, defense). Dumars even failed to draft one of the most talented players in last year's draft, because he already had a player in that position, and he didn't want to disrupt the chemistry of the team. Most teams would have taken that star player anyway and justified it by saying "he was the most talented player available". But for Dumars, players are more than talent. They're about fit.

So my recommendation to all hiring managers, but especially executives, is to embrace the concept of hiring for fit, and getting comfortable saying "no" to a candidate who might make a big splash with the board of directors or Wall Street but who isn't going to make the team better.

How do you do this? There are many great books out there on behavioral interviewing; one of these is *Topgrading* by Bradford D. Smart. But the key is to figure out the one or two behavioral qualities that make someone a good fit for your team, and force yourself to obsess about those qualities when you're sourcing, interviewing, and ultimately, making a hiring decision.

— SUMMER 2004

Five Tips for Better Meetings

It's no secret that most people hate meetings. They find them tedious, unproductive, a waste of time. However, what most people don't realize is that meetings are not inherently bad. We have simply come to accept this is an inevitable truth, and so we get what we expect.

And this is a bigger problem than we realize, because meetings are, in fact, important. They are where CEOs decide whether to open or close a factory, where Presidential cabinets decide whether to wage war or keep peace, where general managers decide which players to trade and which to keep. Regardless of what kind of enterprise or endeavor we're involved in, it's hard to argue that meetings don't matter.

So the big question becomes, "How do we make these things better?" The best way to go about this is to understand the two reasons why meetings usually don't work. First, too many meetings are boring. They are corporate black holes of passion and engagement. Second, too many meetings are ineffective. In spite of the hours we spend in them, we get little closure, resolution or clarity in the end.

Keeping in mind that we're trying to solve both of these problems, here are five tips for changing the way we see and manage meetings.

1. **Know the purpose of your meeting**. Is it about solving a tactical, short-term problem, or a critical strategic issue? Are participants meant to brainstorm, debate, offer alternatives, or just sit and listen? Don't let your meeting devolve into a combination of all of these, leaving people confused about what is going on and what is expected of them.

2. **Clarify what is at stake**. Do participants understand the price of having a bad meeting? Do they know what could go wrong if bad decisions are made? If not, why should they care?

3. **Hook them from the outset**. Have you thought about the first 10 minutes of your meeting and how you're going to get people engaged? If you don't tee up your topic and dramatize why it matters, you might as well invite participants to check-out.

4. **Set aside enough time**. Are you going to be tempted to end the meeting before resolution has been achieved? Contrary to popular wisdom, the mark of a great meeting is not how short it is, or whether it ends on time. The key is whether it ends with clarity and commitment from participants.

5. **Provoke conflict**. Are your people uncomfortable during meetings and tired at the end? If not, they're probably not mixing it up enough and getting to the bottom of important issues. Conflict shouldn't be personal, but it should be ideologically emotional. Seek out opposing views and ensure that they are completely aired.

These five tips alone can improve the quality of our meetings, both in terms of the experience itself as well as the outcome. And considering the almost universal lethargy and disdain for meetings, they can transform what is now considered a painful problem into a competitive advantage.

— SPRING 2004

 The content from this article was based on Pat's book, *Death by Meeting*. For more information on the book, model and free tools, please visit www.tablegroup.com.

Overcome Team Dysfunction

Building an effective cohesive team is extremely hard. But it is also simple. What I mean is that teamwork doesn't require great intellectual insights or masterful tactics. More than anything, it comes down to courage and persistence.

The rewards of teamwork are hard to measure because it impacts the outcome of an organization in such a comprehensive manner, which is impossible to isolate a single variable. As a result, leaders tend to look for more verifiable competitive advantages elsewhere. Although effective teamwork continues to be elusive for most, its power cannot be denied. When people come together and set aside their individual needs for the good of the whole, they can accomplish what might have looked impossible on paper. They do this by eliminating the politics and confusion that plague most organizations. As a result, they get more done in less time and with less cost.

The true measure of a team is that it accomplishes the results that is test out achieve. To do that on a consistent, ongoing basis, a team must overcome the five dysfunctions listed below:

THE FIVE DYSFUNCTIONS OF A TEAM

Dysfunction #1: Absence of Trust

This occurs when team members are reluctant to be vulnerable with one another and are unwilling to admit their mistakes, weaknesses or needs for help. Without a certain comfort level among team members, a foundation of trust is impossible.

Dysfunction #2: Fear of Conflict

Teams that are lacking on trust are incapable of engaging in unfiltered, passionate debate about key issues, causing situations where team conflict can easily turn into veiled discussions and back channel comments. In a work setting where team members do not openly air their opinions, inferior decisions are the result.

Dysfunction #3: Lack of Commitment

Without conflict, it is difficult for team members to commit to decisions, creating an environment where ambiguity prevails. Lack of direction and commitment can make employees, particularly star employees, disgruntled.

Dysfunction #4: Avoidance of Accountability

When teams don't commit to a clear plan of action, even the most focused and driven individuals hesitate to call their peers on actions and behaviors that may seem counterproductive to the overall good of the team.

Dysfunction #5: Inattention to Results

Team members naturally tend to put their own needs (ego, career development, recognition, etc.) ahead of the collective goals of the team when individuals aren't held accountable. If a team has lost sight of the need for achievement, the business ultimately suffers.

THE REWARDS

Striving to create a functional, cohesive team is one of the few remaining competitive advantages available to any organization looking for a powerful point of differentiation. Functional teams avoid wasting time talking about the wrong issues and revisiting the same topics over and over again because of lack of buy-in. Functional teams also make higher quality decisions and accomplish more in less time and with less distraction and frustration. Additionally, "A" players rarely leave organizations where they are part of a cohesive team. Successful teamwork is not about mastering subtle, sophisticated theories, but rather about embracing common sense with uncommon levels of discipline and persistence.

— FALL 2002

 The content from this article was based on Pat's book, *The Five Dysfunctions Team*. For more information on the book, model and free tools, please visit www.tablegroup.com.

About the Author

Patrick Lencioni is the founder and president of The Table Group, a firm dedicated to providing organizations with ideas, products and services that improve teamwork, clarity and employee engagement.

Lencioni's passion for organizations and teams is reflected in his writing, speaking and consulting. He is the author of several best-selling books with nearly three million copies sold. After seven years in print, his book, *The Five Dysfunctions of a Team*, continues to be a weekly fixture on national best-seller lists.

Named in *Fortune* magazine as a 'top ten guru you should know,' Lencioni and his work have appeared in the *Wall Street Journal, USA TODAY, Bloomberg Businessweek, Inc.* and *Harvard Business Review*, to name a few.

When Lencioni is not writing, he consults to CEOs and their executive teams, helping them to become more cohesive within the context of their business strategy. The wide-spread appeal of Lencioni's leadership models have yielded a diverse base of clients, including a mix of Fortune 500 companies, professional sports organizations, the military, non-profits, universities and churches.

In addition, Lencioni speaks to thousands of leaders each year at world class organizations and national conferences. He was recently cited in the *Wall Street Journal* as one of the most sought-after business speakers in the nation.

Prior to founding his firm, he worked as a corporate executive for Sybase, Oracle and Bain & Company. He also served on the National Board of Directors for the Make-A-Wish Foundation of America.

Patrick lives in the San Francisco Bay Area with his wife, Laura, and their four sons, Matthew, Connor, Casey and Michael.

To learn more about Patrick and his firm or to sign up for his POV, please visit www.tablegroup.com.

The Table Group's Products & Services

The Table Group is dedicated to helping organizations of all kinds function more effectively through better leadership, teamwork and overall health.

CONSULTING:

Table Group Consultants employ the 'naked' approach in all their consulting and training engagements. With a variety of service offerings, all sessions are practical, fast-paced and application oriented.

SPEAKING:

Patrick Lencioni brings his models on teamwork, leadership and organizational health to tens of thousands of leaders each year.

BOOKS:

Patrick Lencioni's nine bestselling books have sold nearly three million copies worldwide and tackle topics surrounding organizational health, leadership and teams.

PRODUCTS:

The Five Dysfunctions of a Team and *The Three Signs of a Miserable Job* products were developed to help managers, leaders and their teams address issues around teamwork and employee engagement.

CREDITS

Back cover author photo by James Brian Fidelibus, Photographer

Front cover photo © Ocean/Corbis

Interior photo—odd pages © istockphoto.com/caracterdesign

Interior photo—even pages © istockphoto.com/Nikada

Design by Laurel Katz, izles design